The Book of the People

Also by A. N. Wilson

FICTION

The Sweets of Pimlico
Unguarded Hours
Kindly Light
The Healing Art
Who Was Oswald Fish?
Wise Virgin
Scandal: Or Priscilla's Kindness
Gentlemen in England
Love Unknown
Stray
The Vicar of Sorrows
Dream Children
My Name Is Legion
A Jealous Ghost
Winnie and Wolf
The Potter's Hand

THE LAMPITT CHRONICLES

Incline Our Hearts
A Bottle in the Smoke
Daughters of Albion
Hearing Voices
A Watch in the Night

NON-FICTION

A Life of Sir Walter Scott: The Laird of Abbotsford:
A Life of John Milton
Hilaire Belloc: A Biography
How Can We Know?
Landscape in France
Tolstoy
Penfriends from Porlock: Essays and Reviews, 1977–1986
Eminent Victorians
C. S. Lewis: A Biography
Paul: The Mind of the Apostle
God's Funeral: A Biography of Faith and Doubt in Western Civilization
The Victorians
Iris Murdoch As I Knew Her
London: A Short History
After the Victorians: The World Our Parents Knew
Betjeman: A Life
Our Times: The Age of Elizabeth II
Dante in Love
The Elizabethans
Hitler: A Short Biography
Victoria: A Life

THE BOOK
OF THE PEOPLE
How to Read the Bible

A. N. WILSON

Atlantic Books
London

First published in hardback in Great Britain in 2015 by
Atlantic Books, an imprint of Atlantic Books Ltd.

This paperback edition published in Great Britain in 2016 by Atlantic Books.

10 9 8 7 6 5 4 3 2 1

A CIP catalogue record for this book is available
from the British Library.

Paperback ISBN: 978 1 84887 961 4
E-book ISBN: 978 1 78239 637 6

Printed and bound by
CPI Group (UK) Ltd, Croydon, CR0 4YY

Atlantic Books
An Imprint of Atlantic Books Ltd
Ormond House
26–27 Boswell Street
London
WC1N 3JZ

www.atlantic-books.co.uk

For
Susie Attwood

Whatever's written in what poets name
The book of the people...

W. B. Yeats, 'Coole Park and Ballylee, 1931'

CONTENTS

A PROLOGUE

THE BIBLE USED to be familiar to almost everyone in the Western world, even (I was going to write 'especially') to the illiterate. Visit any great church from Durham to Constantinople, from Rome to Jerusalem, and your eye will fall on images drawn from the Bible, which would have been instantly recognized by any visitor when these places were first constructed. There is Abraham, offering his son Isaac in sacrifice, and having his hand stayed by an angel even as he lifts a knife to the child. There is Daniel in the Lion's Den. There is Noah in the Ark, and there is Noah having landed the Ark, lying in a state of drunkenness. For hundreds of years, the human race filled its mind with these Bible-based images.

With the invention of printing, and the coming of the Reformation, the Bible, translated out of its original Hebrew and Greek into German, English, French, and eventually all the languages of the globe, became what it had never quite been until then: primarily a book, an object which people read as a text. Before that, many people heard the Bible, and saw images taken from it, carved in stone, or painted on glass. But it was not primarily an object, certainly not a book they would have had in their own home. Then came Luther's sublime idea that every ploughboy should be able to read and understand the Scriptures. And from that idea sprang many unforeseen consequences – perhaps the Enlightenment itself, and the eventual decision, by many who read the Book, that it was not true, or not true in the way which they had been taught.

People still went on reading the Bible, however, even in this time of crisis. The Bible would have been read to them in schools. Infant plays based on Daniel in the Lion's Den, or Noah's Ark, or the Nativity of Jesus, would still have been part of their lives, as would at least a selective reading of the Bible texts.

For many people in the Western world today, this is no longer the case. The Bible, for them, is largely unfamiliar. Even those who have attended schools where there is some rudimentary Bible reading in the morning assembly will find, when they visit the great monuments of the Christian past, or read Christian classics such as *Paradise Lost* or Dante's *Divine Comedy*, that the multitudinous Biblical references ring no bells.

It is a bit late in history to say how sad this is – though of course it is sad. One of the reasons for it has perhaps been a tendency, since the Enlightenment towards the close of the eighteenth century, to think of the Bible in fundamentalist ways. The non-believers are more likely, in my view, to have been fundamentalist than the believers. It is the non-believer who tends to think the Bible is 'untrue' because archaeology provides no evidence for the existence of Noah's Ark or the Crucifixion.

This book is an attempt to persuade people to read the Bible. It is not intended to be a contentious book, and it is certainly not telling you what to think. I have cast it in a semi-fictional form, in which incidents and memories and characters in my own life, and a dialogue with a friend to whom I have given the initial L., are the background of the book. My reason for this is that the Bible, more than most books, forms part of one's life once it is absorbed into the system. It does not remain static, any more than you remain ever the same. Your perspective of it will change with the years. I have been lucky enough to have had time not only to read the Bible, but also to study it sporadically. This has helped me to form impressions which I do not wish to force on anyone, but which some readers might find helpful.

This book is intended as a sort of 'guide' to the Bible – as my semi-fictionalized friend L. was a guide to my own reading. It takes a seven-fold form. In the first chapter, I explain why the Quest for the Historical Jesus, in which I have foolishly indulged myself, is a dead end which can only lead nowhere. The Bible was not written by authors with our sense of historical accuracy. Much of it is deeply literary, by which I mean that passages which appear to be plain narratives are actually reworkings of older passages from other parts of Scripture. The literary history of the Bible makes 'literalism' impossible.

So what sort of book is the Bible? The remaining six chapters of my short book explore answers to this question. The first section of the Bible, known in Hebrew as the Torah (Law), implies that every-thing is fixed and grounded, as Biblical fundamentalists want it to be. But for the Jews who wrote down these books, almost the opposite was the case. The very word 'God' was not quite mentionable. If it was, it was not a noun but a verb. Chapter Two suggests that the Jewish concept of God really was different from that of other peoples.

My third chapter explores the sections of Scripture known as the Prophets. The tradition of Biblical prophecy has led to some of the most extraordinary changes in human society, right down to our own day with the Civil Rights Movement in the United States, the overthrow of Soviet power and the abolition of apartheid in South Africa. The reason that my book is called *The Book of the People* is that the Bible has affected human life. It is not proved or disproved by a sceptic poring over its pages in a study. Rather, it is enacted when people such as Martin Luther King or Desmond Tutu are enflamed by it.

The Writings, or the Holy Wisdom, which inform the third section of the Jewish Scriptures, perhaps have no finer examples than the Book of Job and the Book of Psalms, which I consider in detail. Then I return to the questions which have surrounded the truth or otherwise of the Gospels, since they first began to be read with a sceptical eye in the eighteenth century.

In my final chapter, I return to the idea of the Bible as a Book of the People, and of its traditions being carried along through history, not by its quiet existence on a library shelf, but by the living tradition of human beings, who have heard, and acted upon, its words since the first handing-down of the traditions. In this last chapter, I go to Ghent and look at one of the most stupendous readings of the Bible ever undertaken – the Altarpiece, based on the Apocalypse of John. For there are more ways of reading than by merely turning the pages of a book.

ONE

THIS MOUNTAIN

She hears, upon that water without sound,
A voice that cries, 'The tomb in Palestine
Is not the porch of spirits lingering.
It is the grave of Jesus, where he lay.'

Wallace Stevens, 'Sunday Morning'

L. HAD SAID — If you're going to Israel, you've got to see Nablus. You'll see Roman remains, she said, a great colonnade; and you'll see Mount Gerizim towering above the old town. In legendary times, before King David, before the land divided into the northern Kingdom of Israel and the southern Kingdom of Judah, this was Israel's cultic centre. Shechem is its name in the Bible. Then the centre shifted to Mount Zion and Jerusalem, and the people who were left behind, clinging to the old faith, were called Samaritans.

L. and I over the years–

Yes, but who the L.? writes my editor in the margin of the typescript. I see her point. But, by the end of this story, you will know enough about L. Enough. Not very much, but enough. That, by the way, will be one of the points of this book: how much knowledge is enough?

But it is not a book about L. It's a book, in part, about what we have done to ourselves, as a culture either by neglecting the Bible or by making it into an offensive weapon with which to attack people with whom we disagree. L. was the one who was meant to be writing a book about the Bible, but this never came to anything. So in the end, I have decided to write my own version, incorporating some of the things she taught me. I don't know whether she would agree with the conclusions – but that isn't very important.

Back to Israel – in, I suppose, May 1991, when, on L.'s recommendations, we were driving to Nablus on a hot day. R. and I had been together for a couple of years, but still did not know one another very well. We had not yet married. Our companions were K. B., a young colleague on the newspaper where I worked, and his wife B. We were in Israel combining a holiday with a visit to K. B.'s mother, who, though Irish and non-Jewish, had come with a fairly recent husband to live at Jaffa/Joppa, a smart southern suburb of Tel Aviv, better known to the outside world for its oranges. At the party given to celebrate our arrival, we had been shown into a room which seemed to contain all the famous Israelis you'd ever heard of – Daniel Barenboim, Amos Oz, and so on. And now, family visits done, we had checked into the American Colony Hotel in Jerusalem, and were doing some sightseeing.

The car-hire firm had given some confusing, though not, at the time, particularly alarming advice about number plates. If we were going to Jewish areas, it would be safer to have such-and-such a number plate. And if we were going to the occupied West Bank?

Don't go to the West Bank, was the advice.

But I wanted to see Nablus. I had been to Israel quite often before.

I was of the generation where non-Jewish European students went to work on kibbutzim in their gap year. I'd done this after leaving boarding school in 1969 – I'd picked oranges at the Kibbutz Beit HaEmek, near Acre, explored crusader ruins, hitch-hiked through the Negev, smoked on the beach with hippies at Eilat before it was the huge holiday resort it is today, and seen the Biblical sites. I'd stayed for two weeks in Jerusalem at the Anglican cathedral, St George's; I'd visited the Dome of the Rock, the Garden of Gethsemane and the Holy Sepulchre, taken buses to Galilee, seen Nazareth, Capernaum, Bethsaida and Tiberias. But I had never been to Nablus.

The name is an Arabic rationalization of the Greek 'Neapolis'. It was a Hellenistic city, with splendid remains; and it was also in the heart of Biblical Samaria. As we bowled along in the boiling heat, there were many jokes about Good Samaritans, telephoning the Samaritans if we were not enjoying our holiday, and so forth.

Nablus is near the old Biblical site of Shechem, which was a flourishing Canaanite city in the second millennium BC (as recorded in Judges, Chapter 9). According to the old tales, recorded in Genesis, Abraham, our Father in Faith, had a theophany, a vision of God, at Shechem, and built an altar. His grandson Jacob (Israel) did the same [Genesis 33:18–20]. At some point in the early history of Israel, the people who worshipped God at Shechem broke away from those who worshipped God at Jerusalem. If you are a Samaritan, you would probably rewrite that sentence, that the worshippers at Jerusalem were the ones who broke away, while the Samaritans stayed loyal to the Abrahamic faith in Shechem. Certainly by 330 BC, in the Hellenistic period, Shechem was a great city, with a temple. It was laid waste in 107 BC by the Hasmonean John Hyrcanus, so by the time Jesus went there, it would have been a place which had seen better days. The Samaritans, however, are distinctive among the peoples mentioned in the Bible in that they alone, apart from the Jews and the Christians, survive as a separate religious entity to this day. They still maintain the old faith.

L. (who was a Presbyterian) had an affection for the Old Believers whenever they cropped up in Russian literature. (These were the sectarians who refused some very minor innovations in the Russian Orthodox Church in the eighteenth century and thereafter lived slightly outside the ordinary run of society.) She also sympathized with Roman Catholics who yearned for their Tridentine Latin Mass. And she claimed that she had once made a pilgrimage to Sussex to meet the very last of a seventeenth-century sect called the Muggletonians, who got it in the neck from Cromwell, and had been quietly waiting for the Second Coming ever since. They were quite a sizeable sect in Cromwellian days, but by the time L. met them, there were only two left. The Samaritans were her sort of people. One of her favourite sayings was, 'The majority is always wrong'. Sometimes, she'd vary this by quoting the Willie Raskin song, 'Fifty Million Frenchmen Can't Be Wrong'. To which she would add, 'Oh, yeah?' (L. was American.)

It would seem as if the origin of the schism between Samaritans and Jews was simple conservatism. The Samaritans resented innovations being imported into the faith from Jerusalem. They had/have stricter dietary laws, and stricter Sabbath observance than the Jews.

They venerate Mount Gerizim as a place where the God of Israel appeared long before he lighted upon Mount Zion in Jerusalem.

The encounter between Jesus and a woman of Samaria at Jacob's Well [John 4] has no parallels in the other three Gospels. It tells of Jesus sitting by the well when the woman came to draw water. Jesus asked her for water to drink, and she was surprised that a Jew should ask this of a Samaritan, since Jews and Samaritans were on such bad terms.

Jesus then told her that, if she knew who he really was, who had asked her for a drink, then she would be asking him for water – living water. 'The woman said to him, "Sir, you have no bucket and the well is deep. Where do you get that living water? Are you greater than our ancestor Jacob, who gave us the well, and with his sons and his flocks drank from it?" Jesus said to her, "Everyone who drinks of this water will be thirsty again, but those who drink of the water that I will give them will never be thirsty."' [John 4:11–14]

Anyone acquainted with the narrative of the Fourth Gospel will see here something very typical. It has been announced to us in the Preface that Jesus is the Eternal Logos or Word, who took human flesh and walked this earth unrecognized except by a few initiates. In some of the encounters, he gives a 'sign' (which is the word this Gospel uses more than 'miracle') of his true identity and God is thereby glorified. In others, the dramatic irony is preserved, as in this conversation with the Samaritan woman. She does not know who he is. She does not realize, when he speaks of the abundant, living water which he is offering her, that he is speaking symbolically. This is one who has already, in the course of this narrative, transformed water into wine, as a sign of the superabundance of God's grace.

The prophet Jeremiah had spoken of God himself as the fountain of living water [Jeremiah 2:13] and it is this, access to the living God, which Jesus offers. Indeed, later in the conversation, Jesus reveals to us (the initiated readers) just who he is. The woman says that when the Messiah comes, he will reveal himself. 'Jesus said to her, "I am he, the one who is speaking to you."' [John 4:26] The ancient Greek word *eimi* just means 'I am'. But in Hebrew, the great I AM is the word for God himself. The frequent use of the word by the Jesus of the Fourth Gospel proclaims him as the authentic mouthpiece of the living God.

Those with an interest in the geography of the New Testament note that the Fourth Gospel is alone in making Jesus journey through Samaria and have this discussion with a Samaritan. There are probably good reasons for this. One reason could well be that the author is using as his source the earlier Gospels, and the Acts of the Apostles. The Book of Acts, perhaps written some time in the mid-AD 80s, speaks of the first Christians, Jews of Jerusalem, being persecuted by their fellow Jews and scattering to the countryside 'of Judea and Samaria' [Acts 8:1]. Acts speaks frequently either of the Church or of the Word moving first through Biblical Palestine, and then further out, through present-day Syria and up into Asia Minor (modern Turkey). In Acts, there survives the tradition of some in Samaria being converted to the Way of Christ. Probably what is happening in the narrative of Jesus and the woman at the well, in the Fourth Gospel, is that some backdating has gone on: Jesus, who is not recorded as having been to Shechem in Matthew, Mark or Luke, is here made to follow the progress of his church. By AD 90 or 100 – whenever this Gospel was written – the Word has reached

Samaria; the Samaritans, some of them, have drunk of the Living Water.

In this narrative, Jesus and the woman then moved to some of the most basic questions which can be asked of any religion:

> The woman said to him, 'Sir, I see that you are a prophet. Our ancestors worshipped on this mountain, but you say that the place where people must worship is in Jerusalem.' Jesus said to her, 'Woman, believe me, the hour is coming when you will worship the Father neither on this mountain nor in Jerusalem. You worship what you do not know; we worship what we know, for salvation is from the Jews. But the hour is coming, and is now here, when the true worshippers will worship the Father in spirit and truth, for the Father seeks such as these to worship him. God is spirit, and those who worship him must worship in spirit and truth.' [John 4:19–24]

The Fourth Gospel is here in tune with the earliest Christian writings, those of St Paul. First came Judaism – but Judaism, though it had validity in the past, was too wedded to literalism. The revelation of what lay behind the old Bible stories has only been made plain in Christ. Of the Samaritan position, we learn little in the Synoptic Gospels, giving some readers to speculate that the Fourth Gospel has a Samaritan origin, perhaps from Shechem/ Nablus itself. Others place all the writings associated with the name John, the so-called Johannine writings, further west in Asia Minor, perhaps Ephesus.

The drive was fun, the May day light, hot but airy. The centre of Nablus, as we drove round and round trying to find the Church of the Holy Well, was pitted with potholes, and we began to wonder whether we knew the Arabic for 'broken axle', 'flat tyre', 'wrecked car', 'do you take credit cards', or 'please get me out of here'. When we had parked, we sat for a while smoking outside a café, nibbling delicious intensely sweet *kanafeh*, a bright orange pastry crammed with honey-sweetened cheese, and drinking Turkish coffee. The waiter put us in the right direction for the church, which was an easy walk away.

If you are not Orthodox, the experience of entering a church of the Eastern rite is always exotic, but confusing. Should one bow, light tapers, cross oneself from right to left, rather than left to right as Westerners do? Or should one admit difference? Is that murmuring and chanting simply a priest praying, or is there some kind of service in progress?

Nothing was 'going on' in the church today, and a young priest, immediately recognizing us as European visitors, approached and told us the story of Jesus at the well.

While we showed reverence, the young priest went on to tell us the story of the Orthodox priest who had been martyred in the church as recently as 1979. Father Philumen had been standing beside the altar, near Jacob's Well, when fanatical Israeli settlers burst into the church. They had visited a week before, demanding that all Christian symbols – crosses and icons – which had been given by God to Jacob be removed from 'their' Holy Well. On this visit, they were not content to abuse the priest verbally. His mutilated body was later found by the congregation. The fingers of his right hand, with which he would have crossed himself, had been chopped off, and as well as being stabbed, he had been beaten. Although the police were summoned, no one was ever prosecuted for his murder.

The story was painful on many levels. Clearly, the persecution of the Christians in Israel since 1945 was a reality. One of 'our' (C of E) churches in Jerusalem had been burned to the ground and the Israeli fire brigade had been mysteriously slow to come with the hosepipes. On the other hand, these stories – with which you get regaled at all the Christian shrines in Israel/Palestine – of Israeli encroachment on church property, for example – are tinged with a curdled anti-Jewish hatred. We had just been entertained, only days before, by the crème de la crème of liberal Israel, and it was odious to be reminded of the evil things which human beings did to one another because of disputes about the Bible. The debate between the woman at the well and Jesus had here been translated into a modern splurge of ignorant hatred between two groups who disputed the other's reading of God's Book. There was the added pain of not knowing how much of the young priest's story was true. Father Philumen had been murdered – it was an acknowledged fact. But he is now a canonized saint, and any attempt to get to the forensic truth of the case would seem, to one side, to be blasphemous intrusion, and to the other, creepily anti-Jewish.

Quietened by the sad experience of visiting Jacob's Well, we returned to the car, thinking we should be able to see the fine Roman colonnade which L. had recommended, and then maybe have a bite of lunch. But a small crowd had gathered round the car – of boys and youths. The car-hire man had either not properly explained the drill over number plates, or we had not been listening. More likely, we should have heeded his advice not to go into the West Bank with an Israeli car and an Israeli number plate.

The two women of the party were sensible enough to get into the car immediately, and to urge the two men to do the same. Both educated at English boarding schools, the men – K. B. and I – thought we could smile and charm and be patronizing to the protesters who were, after all, only boys. But as the stones started to hurtle in our direction, we followed the wise example of the women and got into the car. My journalist colleague was at the wheel, and after reversing into what felt, not like a pothole, but a volcanic crater, lurched forward again with splutters of the engine, clouds of white dust and a mechanical clanking from behind which made it perfectly possible (if we were judging by hearing alone) that the back of the car containing B. and R. had actually been left on the road. We all drove off, however, with the stones and bricks pelting the sides of the car. Luckily, none hit the windscreen, and we were soon out of town on the dusty road. The Biblical landscape, with Arab shepherds driving their flocks over scrubland, and fudge-coloured hills rolling on either side, took us back again, through what seemed like David Roberts prints or aquatint illustrations of our childhood Gospel-books, to the troubled city of Jerusalem, to a long soak in the bath followed by an even longer soak in the bar. The appalling hatred inspired by the Bible, and by human beings' conflicting readings of the Holy Book, had been on raw display.

As always when visiting Israel/Palestine, the mind returned to the ancient, churning questions of how This turned into That.

For most non-Christians, the puzzle is a very simple one. They can understand that there was once a very holy, wise prophet in Palestine, who attracted a number of followers and who taught them – out of his own Jewish tradition – a new way of living: to live without a sense of self, to abandon concepts of hierarchy, to discard wealth, to eschew violence. They can understand why, when this prophet died, some of his followers collected together his sayings and how, eventually, there were books written which described his dedicated life of teaching and healing. Apparently, he died at the time of the Jewish Passover, during the procuratorship of a notoriously cruel and repressive Roman governor – Pontius Pilate. Like thousands of criminals in the Roman world, he died the hideous death of crucifixion. His followers took the sign of the cross as an emblem in his memory. It became, not merely something by which they remembered Jesus, but an emblem of what he had stood for: the death of self, leading to a resurrection, a new life.

All this can be understood by anyone, whatever their religious background or set of beliefs. What non-Christians (and today, very many Christians) find truly impossible to understand is how this crucified prophet could be claimed as a divine being. One way of explaining this development is to point out that Jesus lived in the eastern Mediterranean, during an era of polytheism. There were many gods. One of the early Christian writers, Luke, describes an incident in a city of Lycaonia, Lystra. Two of the early Christians, Paul and Barnabas, healed a lame man who had previously lost the use of his feet. The excitable crowds 'shouted in the Lycaonian language,

"The gods have come down to us in human form!" Barnabas they called Zeus, and Paul they called Hermes, because he was the chief speaker. The priest of Zeus, whose temple was just outside the city, brought oxen and garlands to the gates; and the crowds wanted to offer sacrifice.' [Acts 14:11–13]

Surely something of the kind must have happened in the case of Jesus – only not in his lifetime, but after his death? The Jews had only One God, and for them it would have been unthinkable that a prophet from among their own number could be a god. But once the news of Jesus spread among non-Jews, and once Paul took the message to places such as Lystra – where you could be proclaimed a god merely for curing someone's lame feet – the atmosphere was different. In the hothouse of first-century pagan Asia Minor, was it not natural that the Christian cult – decades after the real Jesus had left the scene – should have made him into a god?

Certainly, there have been many people – both scholars and well-meaning amateurs – who have read the history of Christianity in this way. Part of their difficulty rests in the fact that there is next to no historical evidence for what the actual Jesus was like. There is a tradition about Jesus, which we first read in the Letters of Paul (AD 50s and early 60s) and which was written down in the form of Gospels in the period AD 70–100. But very little of this material would be of use to a secular historian. No one in the ancient world would have understood exactly what we mean by dispassionate history. It is very important to understand this if one is to make any sense of the strange history of Christianity. There have been many people who have tried to reconstruct the historical Jesus, from the four Gospels in the New Testament, and from the very scanty evidence which exists about Judaism in the first century. But the trouble here is how do you decide which bits of evidence are 'authentic' and which are elaborations, or distortions, or downright inventions? At the time of the Enlightenment in Europe and America, the answer to this seemed rather simple. Thomas Jefferson, for example, in *The Philosophy of Jesus* and *The Life and Morals of Jesus of Nazareth*, wrote a rationalists' 'Gospel', which involved the easy exercise of removing from the story all the miracles. Seventy years later, Lev Nikolaevich Tolstoy, having written the great fictional masterpieces *War and Peace* and *Anna Karenina*, did something similar to Jefferson in Russia, reducing Christianity, and the Gospels, to a compendium of pacifist teachings and removing all references to miraculous healings, as well as to appearances by angels, the rising of Jesus from the dead, or the pouring out of the Spirit upon his followers. Many Americans and Europeans found Jefferson's version of Christianity much more reasonable than the old version, and used the Bible, thereafter, as a compendium of old writings, some of which could help us to live a good life, but much of which clearly belonged to an antiquated, lost way of looking at the world. Likewise in Russia, and throughout the world, millions of men and women were inflamed with Tolstoy's distillation of Jesus's teachings about peace and about the discarding of possessions. Mahatma Gandhi, then a young lawyer in South Africa, was one of those who put these teachings into practice: the radical programme of passive resistance to the British Empire, which led to the eventual ending of the Raj in India, was a direct consequence of Tolstoy's work.

Is it not altogether more rational, if we are attracted to the teachings of Jesus, to follow some such line of approach – to discard any attempt to get our minds around the extraordinary claims made by the earliest Christian writers? For example, in the version of the Fourth Gospel which is read aloud each Christmas, it is stated that 'He was in the beginning with God. All things came into being through him' [John 1:3].

How could such a saying possibly be true? How could it mean anything? How could it be possible to subscribe to a creed which stated that a prophet, who had died by crucifixion some time in the 30s of our era, should have been, not merely 'a god' – as the people in Lystra thought Paul was 'a god' – but, a staggering claim, God himself?

One answer to this could, naturally, be that Jesus himself went about making this claim, and that this was why he was killed – for blaspheming the beliefs of his fellow Jews, who only believe in One God. Versions of this idea resurface throughout Christian history, but a sober reading of the New Testament does not really allow us to believe this. For a start, crucifixion is a Roman method of execution, and no one would have been crucified simply for expressing a view of himself which contradicted Jewish teachings. Secondly, the Gospel writings do not quite allow us to say that Jesus did claim to be God. Rather, they are written by those who revere Jesus as Lord. They are well on the way to believing the full creed of the later Church, that Jesus was 'God from God, light from Light, True God from True God'. In the earliest Gospel, Mark, for example, we read of a healing story, in which Jesus pronounces the forgiveness of a paralytic man's sins. The scribes object – does he not know that no one can forgive sins but God? Jesus replied by asking, '"Which is easier, to say to the paralytic, 'Your sins are forgiven,' or to say, 'Stand up and take your mat and walk?' But so that you may know that the Son of Man has authority on earth to forgive sins" – he said to the paralytic – "I say to you, stand up, take your mat and go to your home.'" [Mark 2:9–12]

In other words, Jesus was performing the acts of God, both when he healed the body *and* when he pronounced forgiveness to the soul. In the Fourth Gospel, the idea of Who Christ Was (what is known as Christology) has developed further. In the passage we have just quoted about Jesus at the well, the woman says that she awaits the Messiah, to which he replies, 'I am he, the one who is speaking to you' [John 4:26]. The ancient Greek *eimi* for 'I am' is also the word for the unutterable name of God, pronounced long ago to Moses from the Burning Bush.

Talking – and writing – to L. about these things after our visit to Nablus, I confided in her my desire to see if I could not somehow make an attempt to recover or reconstruct the historical Jesus.

There was a long sigh.

—You know that's not possible! she said. —The Gospels are all books which were written, by their own account, on the testimony of eye-witnesses to the life of Jesus. But they are not written *by* the eye-witnesses. They are written, therefore, by the next generation down – by, as it were, the grandchildren of Jesus's contemporaries. The testimony which they carry, and which they wish to be passed on through the generations, is nothing less than the Christian faith. That is their task in writing the Gospels. They are written from the point of view of those who already held certain very clear beliefs about Jesus. But they are not modern biographies, still less works of modern investigative history. Nobody was extant, in the years AD 30–90 or 100, to say 'Jesus said such and such, but I have been to Rome and interviewed the followers of Peter; I have been to Antioch and met the grandchildren of the first Christians and I can tell you otherwise. . .' That is the way a modern historian or journalist would go to work, but no such evidence was ever collected or written down. Therefore, however much we try to sift through the New Testament writings for such 'evidence' of what really did or did not happen, we are not going to find very much to help us.

What all the writings provide, in abundance, L. continued, is the faith of the early Church, the faith of the Christians. This written evidence first comes to us from Thessalonica, from Galatia (roughly the location of the present-day capital of Turkey, Ankara) and from Rome. Some of it probably comes from Palestine, where Jesus actually lived, but of that we can be much less certain. None of these documents provide more than fragmentary hints of what the actual historical Jesus did or said except in so far as these sayings and doings relate to later Christian faith. They are gifts to the future generations – but they are the gifts of an inherited tradition of faith. They are not 'research materials': they are the living words of an already existing tradition, which worships Christ as redeemer.

Of course I knew that L. was right. But I was in a curious mood just then. Rather than listening to L.'s objections, I had set out on my own quest for the real Jesus, first by writing a book, and then by translating what I'd written into the form of a television programme.

Making a documentary film about the historical Jesus was a challenge. The idea had arisen because I had been asked by a publisher to write a book on the subject. Against my better judgement, I had said yes. Why against my better judgement? Because I had once read theology at Oxford, and I knew that such a task was impossible. The Quest for the Historical Jesus had always proved illusory to scholars in the past, ever since, in the early nineteenth century in Germany, they had begun to believe it was possible, by painstaking research, to find out the unvarnished historical truth about a non-mythologized Jesus.

When the book was finished, and we thought up a title for the television programme – 'Jesus Before Christ' – the full nature of the misconception should have become clear.

Why is it a misconception?

Many of us, programmed by reading history and journalism, and by following stories on TV or radio news bulletins, suppose that it should be possible, even from the fragmentary materials which exist, to reconstruct what actually happened, who Jesus actually was, how he related to the Judaism of Galilee in his own day, whether he made any 'claims' for himself, or whether these were invented afterwards by myth-makers. But that is the sort of evidence which the New Testament simply does not offer to us. You get no more evidence about the historical Jesus from reading the New Testament than you would if you opened the door of a church in, let us say, present-day Thessalonika, and heard the curious chantings of the Orthodox liturgy. If you were not Orthodox, the words, the music, the enigmatic movements of the priests, the incense rising before the icons would all be incomprehensible. But here is the living Christian tradition. In these chants, in these repetitions of words from Scripture, in these stylized sacred pictures which adorn the walls and the screens, in these lighted candles, is a retention of the mysterious thing which the New Testament also contains: namely the Christian faith. If you entered the church with an Orthodox friend, they would no doubt be able, little by little, to explain to you what was going on, why men in strange robes were appearing and disappearing behind the doors, why they were bowing to the pictures, or waving incense.

It is a little like this when we read the New Testament. Because we read it in modern English, we might suppose that we understand it, and that it is a collection of 'historical' writings, almost accidentally encrusted with 'legends' or bits of esoteric philosophy or mythology culled from the paganism of the first-century world. We might suppose that we could understand it by processes of dissection. In fact, the understanding can never grow unless, as in the middle of a baffling foreign liturgy, we allow *it* to speak to *us*, rather than imposing *our* prejudices and presuppositions upon *it*.

The collection of documents which comprise the New Testament are all very mysterious. I am not referring here to the fact that academic writers puzzle over them. Their task is a special one, calling for a knowledge of ancient languages and cultural history which only a very few would be able to acquire in a lifetime. By saying that the New Testament is mysterious, I am saying something much simpler. To any of us who might open its pages, just as to any of us who pushes open the door of a Christian church to this day, there are mysteries to be experienced. There are stories and images of Christ – just as there are in a church building. But there is precious little 'evidence'. There is a haunting music, which, if our inward ear is attentive, harmonizes with something we already knew. There is a personal appeal, without which the whole enterprise would be mere archaeology, mere antiquarianism. By personal appeal, I mean personal. Those who read the New Testament, or who confront the Christian tradition through the liturgies of the Church, or through observing Christian lives, will soon start to realize that they are not merely encountering a set of rules or a set of stories. The pages of the book, like the buildings of a church, are inhabited. An encounter is about to take place. . .

If you do not believe the Christian tradition – that Jesus was Christ, that Jesus left behind his everlasting presence in the Church, in the Blessed Sacrament of Bread and Wine, that Jesus was the Word Made Flesh – then it seems reasonable, as stated above, to believe that the Church invented this 'theological' Christ out of its memories of a real Galilean prophet who left behind some marvellous teachings, parables about brotherly love and examples of unselfishness. This way of thinking about Jesus was popular in the practical, sceptical nineteenth century. Inspired by such Enlightenment thinkers as Thomas Jefferson, a whole series of different nineteenth-century writers came up with a Jesus in whom a rationalist could believe. David Friedrich Strauss, of the University of Tübingen, made a critical study of the Gospels, and eventually wrote *The Life of Jesus*, which was translated into English by Marian Evans – known to us as George Eliot. Like so many intellectuals of her age, George Eliot was convinced by Strauss's ability to 'get behind' the original documents of the New Testament and somehow produce the authentic prophet; rather as Victorian architects pulled down medieval buildings, with their encrustations of later architectural additions, and put up brand-new, but more authentically 'medieval' Gothic Revival buildings. Strauss, a tormented Hegelian, had enormous influence in the Protestant world, and was a friend, among others, of Queen Victoria's daughter Princess Alice, whose low spirits and experiences of bereavement led her to lose faith in traditional Christianity. Ernest Renan, a French ex-priest, was a more charming writer than Strauss and his *Vie de Jésus* likewise became an international best-seller. It depicted an idealistic rural prophet, persecuted by the ecclesiastical bigots of his day – bigots who, though named Scribes and Pharisees, bore an unsurprising resemblance to the right-wing royalist Ultramontanes who exercised such influence in the French Catholic Church of Renan's day. After a century of writers reconstructing the Historical Jesus, there came Albert Schweitzer with his classic *The Quest of the Historical Jesus*, which made it clear that in looking at what they believed to be Jesus, these well-meaning people were looking down a well and gazing at a reflection of their own faces – or perhaps it would be fairer to Schweitzer to say that they were looking at an image of what they thought best in human nature. Schweitzer himself then provided us with yet another Jesus – perhaps an image of himself? It was of a prophet in despair who believed the world was about to come to an end and who died forsaken by his God.

The trouble with all these Jesuses, as Schweitzer pointed out, is that they were imaginary. In the 1970s, there was another attempt by the scholarly world to reconstruct the historical Jesus, with such attractive books as Geza Vermes's *Jesus the Jew*, and a whole industrial plant, in the American academic scene, of seekers of the historical

Galilean. With the advent of computers as a research aid, it was believed that you could feed in all the known sayings of Jesus and determine which ones were 'authentic'. It was a doomed enterprise. No methodology exists by which you could ever determine whether a story about Jesus is or is not authentic. You believe it is possible that he compared the Kingdom of God to the sower going out to throw seed on the ground, some of which is eaten by birds, some of it choked by thorns, and some growing abundantly (in Mark 4:1–9). This is the sort of story you would imagine a rural Galilean prophet telling, and the Biblical commentaries will tell you that, even if this method of sowing seems wasteful by European standards, it really was practised in the Levant.

But though you might believe this story emanates from Jesus, there is nothing to prove that this is authentic, and the story of, say, his walking on the water in Matthew 14:22–27 is inauthentic, other than your preconceived idea that people just don't walk on water!

The filming was an exhausting experience. We went at the hottest time of the year, and at various junctures everyone in the team became ill. An especially memorable experience was swooping over the whole land of Israel in a helicopter. We were seeing the Land of Promise in a single half-hour, as an eagle or an angel might have seen it – through the Negev, over Jerusalem, up towards Galilee. But as we did so, the charming, hippyish Israeli cameraman, who had been a little tottery from the heat even before the flight began, started to vomit copiously. On another day, after we had been filming for hours in the baking heat at Sepphoris, the Hellenistic city which archaeologists have unearthed just over the valley from Nazareth, first I, and then the English cameraman wilted, and several days of dysentery followed, cured by a gentle old Arab who made us drink sage tea. Simply add boiling water to sage leaves and drink: I recommend it to anyone with the wrenching gut-pains, the endless runs, the near delirium which the condition entails. We were cured almost instantly.

A dazzling array of distinguished scholars had been flown out to take part in the film, including Geza Vermes himself, Ed Sanders, then Professor of New Testament at Duke University, and Paula Fredriksen of Boston University. They all, like me, wanted to plug the idea of the simple Galilean prophet who had been turned into a figure of mythology – by Paul, by the Early Church, by some mysterious process of history.

When you are filming with people, you spend a lot of time together, and more is revealed of oneself than would be the case during, say, a simple academic conference. It struck me that, although we all considered ourselves to be rationalists, we were peddling a story which basically made no sense whatsoever.

Filming had been miserable. Not only had we all been ill, we had been tetchy. There had been squabbles between director and presenter which the wise – actually rather saintly – English cameraman and sound recordist had helped to calm. R. had kindly flown out to console me in my misery, and we decided to return to the American Colony hotel for a few days' holiday before we flew back to England.

Any visitor to Jerusalem must have conflicts of feeling. In my own case, I had visited the city so often that I believed the conflicts to be under control. I thought I was 'mature' enough to live with the multi-faceted palimpsest of the city's history and to recognize that it was inevitable, given the nature of the place and the intensity of beliefs which had been held around it, that hatreds, like briars, should so readily have sprung up.

On this visit, however, we were both overwhelmed by the hatred all around us. Going to the Holy Sepulchre had been a mixed experience: you could sense the seriousness and piety of the pilgrims, and smile indulgently at the Franciscan friars deliberately provoking the Orthodox monks as they stomped around the crusader church, banging their staves on the stone floor. It is said – I think it is true – that the key of the whole church has to be in the custody of a Muslim because the Christians have fought – literally fought – over who had the right to possess it. While we were in Jerusalem that last visit, there was yet another story in the newspaper – was it about an Armenian monk hitting a Copt over the head with a broom, or was it aboiut an Orthodox doing something equally violent to a Copt? The bristling hatred is alive, like some virus, in every spice-fumed alley and every scrubby escarpment of the city. Nor, of course, is the hatred limited to late-classical or medieval Christian feuds, grotesquely perpetrated at the holy sites. At the Al-Aqsa mosque are preserved the blood-stained clothing of the children gunned down by Israeli troops during one of the intifadas. The American Colony is just around the corner from the Palestinian Authority. Towards the end of Saturday, we sat in the garden drinking mint tea when we heard what seemed to be a small riot happening outside the walls of the hotel. We went out to investigate. The hotel janitor told us it happened every week, as the Shabbat ended. A large group of young men – looking as if they had come from a shtetl in Minsk, circa 1870, in wide-brimmed furry hats, black frock coats and some still wearing or holding their fringed prayer shawls – marched through the street, yelling abuse and waving banners.

Back at the hotel, we changed our mint tea to strong whisky. The atmosphere of loathing which the Israeli demonstrators had displayed seemed all of a piece with every other manifestation of human idiocy we had seen and heard: monks hitting other monks with brooms, Muslims hating Jews, fanatical Muslim suicide bombers blowing themselves up at crowded bus stops, etc., etc., etc.

I thought back to the boys who had thrown stones at the car the previous year, in Nablus. Places carry memories in earth, stones and trees. Certain places – for me, the shrine of Apollo at Delphi is such a place, and the shrine at Walsingham – seem afloat with peacefulness. Other places – such as the battlefield of Campaldino which I once visited when researching my book on Dante – still shimmer with menace, as do some of the forts in the Scottish borders where reivers and bandits have fought and killed one another so persistently over the years. Nablus/Shechem has been seething with religious hatred for years. This fact was known, presumably, not only by the author of the Fourth Gospel but by his first audience, a fact which made the encounter between a Jewish healer-prophet and a Samaritan woman at the well so striking. "'Our ancestors worshipped on this mountain, but you say that the place where people must worship is in Jerusalem." Jesus said to her, "Woman, believe me, the hour is coming when you will worship the Father neither on this mountain nor in Jerusalem.'" [John 4:20–21]

After that last visit to Jerusalem – and I feel no inclination to return – I was shell-shocked by the sheer stupid hatred displayed by all sorts of human beings, caused by one thing: religion. I resolved to sit down and try to write a rational book about the Bible. It would surely be possible to put into words a cool, sensible account of how the Bible actually came to be written. This would be the sanest counterblast to the hatred we had so palpably witnessed in the Holy City.

No doubt the religiously based conflicts in the world originated for any number of psychological, historical and sociological reasons. But as far as the People of the Book were concerned, it was all based on fundamental misconceptions about the Bible. The most passionately hate-filled disputes, continuing through generations and centuries, were being fought between people who entertained different views on the Bible. And these views were not based on reasonable difference. The bitterest wars, the bloodiest battles, were fought between people of near-total ignorance.

—You should write a sensible book about the Bible, I told L.

We had met in London at the Museum Tavern. It was before the British Library moved up to the Euston Road, and she had spent the day in the old reading room where Marx wrote *Das Kapital*. I had bought her half a pint of ginger-beer shandy, but she had not done more than sip from it as she puffed on cigarettes. I was drinking red wine.

—*How to Read the Bible*. She laughed. —It sounds too bossy. *How to Read the Bible Sensibly. A Sensible Person's Guide to the Bible.*

—After that last experience of Israel, I replied, I almost wonder whether the Bible should not be banned. Whenever I turn on a television or open a newspaper, there is yet another instance of religion inspiring people to behave, not just badly but insanely. Our ancestors worshiped on this mountain. The Bible says we are entitled to this bit of land. The Bible says women must do that or gays must do the other. Obscure bits of the Bible, perhaps scratched on a piece of papyrus in the second century BC, relating to some Bronze Age myth, were seriously produced, in the United States and Great Britain, as reasons for objecting to medical research, or liberalization of certain laws. Questions about how we could teach our children science are also obscured by arcane twisting of the Bible, to make it a geological or biological textbook, set up in competition against the discoveries of post-1850 scientists.

—Maybe you're too angry to write a book about the Bible. Maybe you should go away and learn a language.

I saw that L. was hurt, but I did not quite understand why.

She was right, I think. No doubt there was a need for a quietly rational book, explaining to these misguided multitudes why they had got the Bible all wrong. But if I was right, and they were all such bigots, who among the fundamentalists would want to read such a book?

It was the period when anti-God literature had started to hit the best-seller lists. There was no God and these angry writers were his prophets. Nearly all my sympathies were with the denouncers.

Salman Rushdie had been condemned to death by the Ayatollah Khomeini in Iran – for writing a novel! I wrote a short, intemperate pamphlet entitled 'Against Religion'. I suppose, in common with most liberal thought in the 1990s, that was my simple position. But nothing is ever simple, and the idea of writing that Bible book did not entirely go away.

THE VULGATE
OF EXPERIENCE

God is not a being, he is being.

Étienne Gilson

IN THE BEGINNING, God. . .

You ask how the Bible is going. Ever thought about it as the primary atheist text?!! So wrote L. on a postcard some time in the 1980s. (The postmark is smudged, and she has written neither address nor date.)

It reminds me, for some reason, of that classic 1922 essay by H. L. Mencken, 'Memorial Service', in which he listed all the dead gods of history. 'Huitzilopochtli is as magnificently forgotten as Allen G. Thurman. Once the peer of Allah, Buddha and Wotan, he is now the peer of General Coxey, Richmond P. Hobson, Nat Petterson, Alton B. Parker, Adelina Patti, General Weyler and Tom Sharkey.' After listing dozens of dead gods, Mencken wrote, 'Ask the rector to lend you any good treatise on comparative religion; you will find them all listed. They were gods of the highest dignity – gods of civilized peoples – worshipped and believed in by millions. All were omnipotent, omniscient and immortal. And all are dead.' (I think 'any good treatise on comparative religion' would probably question the sentence about their omnipotence; but it would have been a pity to spoil a magnificent sentence.) I wonder whether Mencken's article helped to inspire Wallace Stevens's 'Notes Toward a Supreme Fiction':

> The death of one god is the death of all.
> Let purple Phoebus lie in umber harvest,
> Let Phoebus slumber and die in autumn umber,
>
> Phoebus is dead, ephebe. But Phoebus was
> A name for something that never could be named.

When I quoted this once on a card to L., she replied, 'What is this but Justin Martyr's *First Apology in defence of Christians*? No one can give a name to God, who is too great for words; if anyone dares to say it is possible to do so, he must be suffering from an incurable madness.'

In the beginning, there were many gods. Even in the Bible, even in the first five sacred books of the Jews, known as the Torah or the Pentateuch in the Greek version, the traces of these dead gods remain. One of the authors of Genesis has been identified by the letter J because the author worshipped a god called Yahweh (Jahweh, if you were a nineteenth-century German scholar, hence the letter J). Harold Bloom thinks this was a woman, living in the reign of

King Solomon. Others think the J tradition of stories is much later – written down after the Babylonian exile of 597 BC.

Another strand of writing in Genesis names God not Yahweh, but Elohim, and this writer has been known as E. Whereas Yahweh originally was an anthropomorphic God who walked about his garden like a sheikh, spoke to his creatures, lost his temper, decided to scrap the whole of creation and start again, Elohim was a more mysterious God, who communicated with his creation by means of dreams, or messengers (angels).

Another writer whom we can discern at work in Genesis is P, the priestly source. Whereas for J the dominant figure in the story is Abraham, our Father in Faith, for P the hero was Moses, and it was through Moses that God was able to convey to his people the Ten Commandments, given during a theophany on Sinai. To these simple injunctions, P added a host of prescriptions, both of ritual observance and of such matters as diet, how to avoid corpse impurity, when it was permissible during the menstrual cycle for women to indulge in sexual intercourse, and so forth. Another author is the Deuteronomic author, possibly writing in the seventh century BC, whose hand has been detected not only in the Book of Deuteronomy, but in the working of the Laws given to Moses in the desert. These last two authors, P and D, imagined Moses, in the time of Rameses II (mid-thirteenth-century BC), establishing the liturgical and ritual arrangements of the supposed First Temple era (say 962–922 BC), the furnishing of the tabernacle with curtains and screens, for example, the weaving of finely wrought vestments and the burning of incense in elaborate lampstands. They do not explain, however, how Moses, even given his miraculous powers, found the material for these beautiful artefacts in the middle of the desert.

So the sacred books of the Law, which are the most important books in the synagogue, had an origin which was varied in time, place and authorship. They had their origins in a polytheistic world, where there were many gods. Even within primitive Judaism, there is the recognition that Yahweh's people will be constantly tempted to worship gods other than him.

Bible scholarship would seem to be at variance with Jewish orthodoxy here – and probably with Christian orthodoxy. Whereas the orthodox or 'fundamentalist' view of the Torah is that it is God's Word, pure and simple, the scholar would want to say that nothing is simple, and that even to identify the various words for God in the Pentateuch – the Lord, the Most High, and so on – is to muddle deities who in their origins were separate.

But the orthodox, of either Jewish or Christian persuasion, would in a sense be right? Whatever the *origins* of the various stories in the first five books of the Bible, readers are not the same as archae-ologists. To identify the 'God' who walked in the Garden of Eden with the 'God' who appeared to Jacob in a dream, when the angels ascended and descended a ladder set up between heaven and earth, is not to confuse, but to develop. The Bible is not the uncooked ingredients which scholars can identify when they establish, by the process known as Form Criticism, which bits were written by P, which by J and so on. The Bible as we have it today is a whole book, a ragout whose ingredients have been bubbling together for hundreds of years.

However much L. and I disagreed over the years, she had taught me one thing from the beginning about the Bible, and that was

the truth so well enunciated by her mentor – the Canadian critic
Northrop Frye:

> The Bible is held together by an inner core of mythical
> and metaphorical structure: mythical in the story it tells of
> the redemption of man from between the beginning and
> the end of time; metaphorical in the way that its imagery
> is juxtaposed to form an 'apocalyptic' picture of a cosmos
> constructed according to the categories of human creative
> energy (i.e. the animal world appears as pastoral, the mineral
> world as urban etc. . . .). This poetic unity is there: how it got
> there will doubtless always be something of a mystery. . . We
> can only call it a mystery of canonicity, and let it go for the
> time being, holding in the meantime to our central principle:
> the Bible is not a work of literature, but its literal meaning is
> its mythical and metaphorical meaning.

She had also taught me, though I kept forgetting it, that the Biblical
conception of God is unlike the polytheistic sense of 'Gods'. The dead
gods listed by H. L. Mencken are like the false idols so constantly
mocked in the Bible. They are all proper nouns. The true God is a
Verb. The concept of Yahweh, the Great I AM, is closer to Goethe's
'*Das Werdende, das ewig wirkt und lebt*' ('That which is passing into
new being works eternally and lives') than it is like the concept of
an entity. That is why conversations about whether God 'exists' are
always nonsensical.

The Book of the People! The authentic Bible is not the shards,
the bits which textual scholarship might, with greater or lesser

degrees of plausibility, unearth (interesting as the process of investigation is). The authentic Bible, the living Bible, is the collection of different authors which were fused into the redaction now known as the Pentateuch or the Torah. Whatever the raw material was, and however raw it was, the Bible as we know it, and as it has influenced life and literature ever since, is a product of the Axial Age, that pivotal period in human history which at its outset saw the emergence of the great Hebrew prophets Jeremiah and Ezekiel, which saw the arrival of the Lord Buddha, and which also towards its close saw the coming of Plato and the Greek tragedians.

Just as Plato banished the legendary gods and goddesses of Homeric mythology for what they were – myths – so the Bible, that atheist text, as L. called it, banished all Yahweh's rivals. In origin, this might appear to be symptomatic of what so many people, myself included, find so repellent about the Religions of the Book – Judaism, Christianity and Islam all three. In the Bible, Yahweh insists upon his people destroying other people, taking their land, desecrating their sacred buildings and shrines. After Yahweh has led the people through the Sea of Reeds, and the pursuing Egyptians' chariots have stuck in the mud, and the waters have closed over the heads of the Egyptians, Moses sings a blood-curdling song. It is probably one of the oldest passages in the Bible:

> Who is like you, O Lord, among the gods?
> Who is like you, majestic in holiness,
> awesome in splendour, doing wonders?
> You stretched out your right hand,
> the earth swallowed them.

In your steadfast love you led the people whom you redeemed;
you guided them by your strength to your holy abode.
The peoples heard, they trembled;
pangs seized the inhabitants of Philistia.
Then the chiefs of Edom were dismayed;
trembling seized the leaders of Moab;
all the inhabitants of Canaan melted away.
Terror and dread fell upon them;
by the might of your arm, they became still as a stone
until your people, O Lord, passed by...

[Exodus 15:11–16]

Those of us who grew up reading the Bible often, and regularly, sometimes overlook the sheer underlying violence of the monotheistic idea. As we played with our Noah's Ark, and arranged our wooden Mrs Noah next to the pairs of wooden animals, we failed to notice that these lucky dolls were the survivors of a major act of genocide, in which a petulant God had decided that he did not love the human race any longer, and would therefore destroy it by flood. There are many flood myths and legends in the anthropology of the world. But the Biblical one, as edited in the two versions given in Genesis, one by P and one by J, are both exclusive and destructive. It is hard to see how monotheism, in this setting, can be anything else. God's people are saved, spared in the Ark, which for later, Christian generations, became an emblem of the Church. Everyone else, by virtue of not being loved by God, by virtue of worshipping the wrong God, is drowned.

This is the dark side of monotheism. Far from being apologetic about it, the opening books of the Bible, in their monotheistic redactions (of polytheistic texts), whoop with blood-curdling hatred of non-orthodox or non-Yahweh-worshipping neighbours.

The Bible is quite honest about this. On the other hand, the Bible does not stop with the stories of destruction and conquest with which the first six of its books (the Pentateuch and Joshua) are concerned. It also contains the most sublime stories, suggestive of the possibility that men and women are not solely earth-bound creatures. In our dreams, prayers, imagination, we can discover links between the temporal and the eternal.

Jacob left Beer-sheba and went toward Haran. He came to a certain place and stayed there for the night, because the sun had set. Taking one of the stones of the place, he put it under his head and lay down in that place. And he dreamed that there was a ladder set up on the earth, the top of it reaching to heaven; and the angels of God were ascending and descending on it. And the Lord stood beside him and said, 'I am the Lord, the God of Abraham your father and the God of Isaac; the land on which you lie I will give to you and to your offspring; and your offspring shall be like the dust of the earth, and you shall spread abroad to the west and to the east and to the north and to the south; and all the families of the earth shall be blessed in you. . .' Then Jacob woke from his sleep and said, 'Surely the Lord is in this place – and I did not know it!' And he was afraid, and said, 'How awesome is this place! This is none other than the house of God, and this is the gate of heaven.' [Genesis 28:10–17]

This is such a deep story, about the dawning religious imagination of the human race. No wonder that in such glories as the west front of Bath Abbey, carvers and glass-makers so often depicted Jacob's Ladder.

Surely the Lord is in this place – and I did not know it. . . It is the Bible's genius constantly to surprise and remind us of the possibility of finding ourselves in a spot from which angels have ascended and descended.

The close textual criticism of the Bible will at first make us feel the book coming, as it were, apart in our hands, and with it anything even resembling a religious faith. Here, in this story of Jacob's Dream, for example, we find various elements at work, which are not completely apparent in the amalgam which constitutes the present text of Genesis. The original of the folk-tale clearly has Jacob arriving at the holy place at nightfall. It is already a famous holy place, but because of the dark he does not recognize where he is. E, who shies away from direct human encounters with God, makes Jacob experience the holiness of the site by a revelation of angels. Later, when Jacob wakes up, J makes Yahweh speak to him directly. But as it survives to us in our translated Bibles, it is a story which encapsulates religious experience on the deepest level; it is about the human failure to grasp 'the many splendoured thing', it is about the visionary and imaginative possibilities in human life which much of the time we hold at bay.

But at that phase of my life, during that conversation with L., I was still in righteous hate with the Bible.

—I just hate the way the Bible, for millions of people around the world, remains a work of unique authority. Damn it, it's a poem, a collection of myths! You can't live a poem! And you just can't force other people to live in a poem.

—Many people have, said L.

—But you know what I am talking about! They open the Bible – a collection of texts written thousands of years ago. . .

—Perhaps many hundreds. . .

—And expect other people – this is my quarrel with it – they expect *other people* to live their lives in a particular way because of *their* crazy way of interpreting the Bible.

—What are you talking about?

—I am talking about the support given by American evangelicals to the State of Israel, because they believe 'the Bible says' the land belongs to the Jews – as far up as the River Euphrates! Does that mean these people would encourage an invasion of Iraq?

We were arguing in the earlier part of the 1990s, before that invasion had in fact taken place. I ranted on:

—I am talking about the teaching of science in schools: on the one hand, you have reasonable science teachers trying to teach children geology, biology, etc., and on the other hand, you have these crazies telling the schools they must teach the children that the world only dates back to 4004 BC. And why?

—Because, said L. quietly, Archbishop Ussher, a patient fellow evidently, in the seventeenth century, went through the whole Bible and counted back all the generations in the Bible, from So-and-so begat So-and-so until he got back as far as Adam and Eve, and if you added up all the begats and begats and all the years in between, you got to somewhere like October 4004, which was when the Creation happened, shortly followed by the Fall of Man.

—But you are saying that, L., with an ironic smile on your face, and I am talking about people – millions of people on this planet – who actually *believe* that; who think the Bible teaches them that science is baloney, that gay people are going to hell, that. . .

—I know, I know.

—You know, next year in Jerusalem they are going to celebrate the three thousandth anniversary of the foundation of the city by King David. Now, archaeologists have been working in the Middle East for *years* and they have not found any trace of the City of Zion, founded by King David, nor of the beautiful temple built by his son Solomon. They are legendary characters, not figures in history. Yet the world leaders will solemnly send representatives to endorse this. . . this myth! It's like. . . it's like. . .

Because I was spluttering, L. supplied my need.

—It's like the leaders of the European Union trying to decide whether Turkey should join, and doing so on the basis of reading the *Iliad*. Whereas we think the *Iliad* is – albeit a masterpiece – 'just a poem'. And you are saying the Bible is 'just a poem' and should not be used to decide real issues, like the borders of modern countries in the Middle East, or how to teach science, or whether gays are going to hell.

—Correct.

—Of course, on one level I agree with you.

L. took a drag on her cigarette.

—Of course, it drives me nuts, she said, when people use phrases like 'The Bible says' or 'The Bible teaches' and then use the sacred scrolls as a megaphone through which they can shout their own opinions!

We did not often meet at this period. I was working as a busy journalist and writer in London. L. had a series of jobs, seldom in London, as a supply teacher in British secondary schools (high schools): that is, she never had tenure in a school, but she stood in for teachers who were absent. If a school needed an English teacher for two terms, she would go for two terms; if for only two weeks, likewise. The provisional nature of the work evidently suited her. She wanted to live without attachments, without possessions. She never owned a house or a car or seemed rooted in any particular location. Every now and then she would disappear from my life for a year or two. Sometimes I would learn she had been abroad – a period of study leave, or some scholarship, at an American or European university; a spell in a religious house. I was only dimly aware of her periodic bouts of mental illness – clearly these were not something she wanted to discuss with me. They remained 'off limits'. Most of my inner life was sealed off from her, and even more of hers was sealed off from me. She troubled me, because I knew from the beginning that she was one of those God-stricken people, in love with God, unable to get him out of her system. I found this fact tragic and infuriating and fascinating. I envied it. I knew that because she was God-stricken she was able to read with a particularly heightened imaginative awareness all manner of old texts. Not simply the Bible, but the Christian poetry of Dante and Spenser and Blake made more sense to her than they did to me.

Sometimes I asked her about her book 'How to Read the Bible', which she had been 'writing' ever since I first met her in 1970. Sometimes we would revert to the dialogue of which I have just provided a short snatch, and which continued between us for some thirty-three years.

—You see, the reason I don't agree with you is that you, too, are being a kind of fundamentalist, she would say. —And also, the fundamentalists you so much dislike are right, and you are wrong. The Bible is a book, or collection of books, which does make a demand, which has changed the way whole societies and cultures have thought. To this extent it is different in kind from the *Iliad*.

—You mean, it's more like Mao's *Little Red Book*, or *Das Kapital*.

—In a sense, maybe. Only with a difference... yes, that's it! This difference. They are the works of one author influencing the many. The Bible is the work of the many. You know those mysterious words in Yeats's 'Coole Park and Ballylee, 1931' – 'what poets name / The book of the people'.

—He wasn't talking about the Bible.

—I know he wasn't; but the Bible is not only the work of many hands; and not only has it passed through many different redactors to turn into the single volume we today call 'The Bible'. It has gone on being the Book of the People. Different readers have changed it, not always by literary means. They have taken the Bible and their reading of it has changed the world.

—Or refused to let it change. I mean, look at the Anglican Communion to which I once thought I belonged! Because of the gross homophobia of a few 'fundamentalists', these forty million or so human beings are having the most ridiculous quarrel about homosexuality. In the past, okay, people believed that homosexuality was a sort of mental disease which could be cured. Doctors believed that, not just Bible-bashers. But now, medicine, science, common sense all show that if you are gay, there is nothing whatsoever you can do about it. Yet these people, rather than having a sensible discussion about it, insist on opening their Bibles and finding the few, the very few texts in which homosexuality is mentioned...

—But this is in a way all part of what I want to write about, said L. dreamily.

—What, Anglican gays? Spare us!

She paused and lit up once more.

—This problem you mention is besetting the Protestant world. You despise them for setting so much store by the word of God, as they see the Bible. But think back! Think back to Martin Luther. He translated the Bible into German, at breakneck speed, because he believed that any ploughboy should be as free as the Pope to study and interpret God's word. And after that – POW! From this one exciting act of Luther's sprang the whole modern world outlook. Not just Protestantism, but the scientific outlook, and the Enlightenment. After the German ploughboy had been given his copy of the Bible, no one needed 'authorities' any more, telling them what to think. Here was a book – read it and make up your own mind. But human beings don't really want to make up their own minds – not many of them, not for long. So the Protestants made the Bible into a sort of Pope, an infallible source – and that's where your 'fundamentalists' come from. Meanwhile, the spirit of freedom which Luther unleashed in the sixteenth century, the spirit of inquiry, began to undermine the very freedom felt by the ploughboy. Because by the late eighteenth, early nineteenth century, the heirs of Luther, the German Lutherans, had started to undermine the Bible itself. They investigated how the various books came into being.

They dissected it. They found that much of what had been seen as history was myth; much of what had been believed as literal was figurative. . .

—So, since the German Biblical scholars of the nineteenth century, we can just chuck the Bible – certainly not regard it as infallible?

—Why would you want to chuck it, just because it isn't infallible? You see, this is what is so strange about this modern, growing hatred of the Bible and Christianity, she said calmly. —Here's the book which has been our book – as a civilization, our book – for nearly two thousand years, and for the first time ever in history, the intelligent world has taken leave of it. And because they do not read the Bible, because they do not read it over and over again as their forebears did, and live in it, these anti-Godders and secularists have forgotten, totally, what the experience of reading the Bible is actually like. You are doing it yourself now, boiling the Bible down to a few matters like sex, or the Middle East or science. . .

—They are quite big matters.

—Possibly. But there are also other matters. Who we are, what we are. . .

—You can decide those matters without reading the Bible.

—Of course you can. I am certainly not saying otherwise. But we are missing out when we do so. Also – this is another thing I want to write about, if I ever start the book – is how many of us *think* we are living outside the world of the Bible, merely because we no longer read it. . . 'Transparent man in a translated world'.

—That's rather good. What is it?

She gave me one of her infuriating smiles.

On another occasion, she said:

—The people came first, and the Book came next. The Bible was created by people, and it was handed on by people, and the shape it took was determined by people.

Sometimes, when I had the courtesy to reply to L.'s letters, she would try to articulate what she had been writing. Sometimes she would even send me draft pages. These, from the same period, are from a typescript, across which she has written: 'poss. opening?'

Follow pattern of Bible itself with three broad categories – the Torah, the Prophecies, the Writings. Then explore some of the Writings in more depth – Job, Psalms. By now it should be clear what we are doing. It's not a work of polemic, and it's not really a 'How to Read the Bible' book, either.

Luther's achievement was to encourage the growth of a literate world, our world. But the more literate we became, the more the world came to regard the Bible as a book and only as a book. There have in fact been many ways of 'reading the Bible'. The great cathedral builders were reading the Bible, so were the medieval sculptors and glass-makers and the actors in the mystery plays. Similarly, the abolitionists in the eighteenth century who began the anti-slavery campaigns were inspired by Scripture, but they were not just 'inspired' – plenty of people had used the Bible to justify slavery. The campaigners revivified the Biblical sense of Prophecy. This has happened in our own time. 1968 was a year of prophets, and of prophets being slain. 'Rejoice and be glad – for your reward is great in heaven – for in the same way they persecuted the prophets who were before you.'

All this is a way of reading. You don't just read when you are sitting still and letting your eyes run over a page. You read as you live, you live as you read. When the New Testament came to be written down, it told the story of what it had to say by endless recraftings and rewritings of the Bible. Until it in turn became the Bible. . .

Some such thoughts, anyway!

But begin as the Bible begins. Begin with God, and with the Biblical idea(s) of God.

The utter destruction of Jerusalem in AD 70 remains one of the 'before' and 'after' moments of history. Not only would Judaism never be the same, but human history would never be the same either. The terrible details of the siege of the city, the wholesale slaughter, the starvation of the inhabitants, the hatred visited upon the Jews by the Romans, are all told by the Jewish historian Josephus (37 BC?–AD 100), who bought his freedom by changing sides and was able to live out his days in Rome, writing two works of history: the unforgettable account of the Roman rape of his country, *The Jewish War*, and the more diffuse *The Antiquities of the Jews*.

He was not only popular in late antiquity. He was also the most popular author of the English-speaking eighteenth century. Persecuted Protestantism identified with persecuted Judaism, and if the early colonists in America arrived with any books apart from the Bible, they would as like as not be the works of Josephus. In my Penguin copy of *The Jewish War*, I have just found a note from L.

Am reading Josephus again –

The 'again' was somehow rather annoying!

And thinking about the destruction of the Temple. For the Bible book.

A hundred years before the army of Titus destroyed the city, Pompey invaded it, and violated the Temple by entering the Holy of Holies. I want somehow to work this into the beginning, entering a temple, and getting right in there, to its core, to find the God. In any other temple in the ancient world – when you had gotten past the outside abattoir, and the butchers slaughtering the animals, and the priests or the prostitutes, or both! – you'd have come to the really holy bit: the statue of many-dugged Artemis, or Herakles, or whoever. But in Jerusalem, the great Temple built by Herod had a Sanctuary which had no statue – no God in a sense. THE BIBLE IS THE FIRST ATHEIST TEXT – that's what many people do not realize.

P.S. – I read your intemperate anti-religion pamphlet. Hmmm.

In time – after quite a bit of time – I began to see what L. was saying. As the anti-God 'debate' in the West (or was the debate only happening in the bookstores and television studios of the West?) gathered momentum, the Bible's role in the story seemed ever more crude, with the fundamentalists on both sides failing to see what it actually said – and, literally, 'where it was coming from'.

L.'s book about the Bible – which in those days I still believed was on the verge of completion – was going to be a reading of the Bible from beginning to end. But it was not only going to be an expository work. She was going to explore the way in which the Bible impacted upon history, and upon human lives at different periods; on how the readers of the sacred texts had in various ways altered it.

I know from the letters she wrote at this period that she liked the work of some of the modern 'atheists' while disliking the shriller voices of the others. At the root of much of the quarrel were some quite extraordinarily crude ideas about God.

When L. wrote in capitals, 'THE BIBLE IS THE FIRST ATHEIST TEXT', she was drawing on the bafflement felt by pagans who invaded the Jerusalem Temple, and by many modern unbelievers about the Biblical picture of God.

—They are right to reject these bad arguments for God. They are right to say these Gods do not exist. What they do not realize is that...

—I am of their number, L.! (We were sitting on a bench in Battersea Park, looking at the river.)

—You think you are, because you have been totally disillusioned by the Bible and by Christianity. But you will come through that.

—How do you know?

—In order to come to the truth, you have to discard falsehood, that is the central story of the Bible. There's a poem called 'Les Plus Belles Pages'. Unlike the long discursive poems, you can grasp it quite quickly. It is not the best of Stevens, but it is characteristic. One notes the pretentiousness – why is the title in French? It is perhaps more notes towards a poem than the finished thing.

She then recited it.

> The milkman came in the moonlight and the moonlight
> Was less than moonlight. Nothing exists by itself.
> The moonlight seemed to.
>   Two people, three horses, an ox
> And the sun, the waves together in the sea. [In this line
>   you get the music, the way the best of Stevens sings,
>   said L.]
> The moonlight and Aquinas seemed to. He spoke,
> Kept speaking, of God. I changed the word to man.
> The automaton, in logic self-contained,
> Existed by itself. Or did the saint survive?
> Did several spirits assume a single shape?
>
> Theology after breakfast sticks to the eye.

The last line is another side of Stevens which can irritate – the smart-ass, the epigram which does not quite come off.

In this poem, he projects on to Aquinas his own mindset. ('He spoke, / Kept speaking, of God.') Stevens was one of the most eloquent exponents of modern atheism. (The jury seems to be out about whether, in his last days, he converted to Catholicism. As often happens on these occasions, a hospital chaplain claimed one thing and Stevens's daughter an irate other thing.) In the best of his poems, he sees his function as a remaking of language itself, of understanding how we can speak about experience and hope to describe the thing-in-itself. The exercise is an obstacle course which will lead to perpetual unravelling.

In Stevens's generation, 'Aquinas' was a word which did not

so much stand for the thirteenth-century philosopher, as for the use made of Aquinas's philosophy in the twentieth century. In his lifetime, Aquinas was viewed with some suspicion by many in the Church, because, as you will discover if you dig into the millions of words which he left behind him, he regarded the philosopher's task as to question everything. Absolutely everything.

The neo-Thomists of the twentieth century wanted to make Aquinas into the justification, exemplum, for a philosophical defence of religion. Although Aquinas rejected, for example, the doctrine of the Immaculate Conception of the Blessed Virgin, he was made into a Doctor of the Church by the nineteenth-century Popes, and in the twentieth century, Roman Catholic priests were made – after the so-called Modernist crisis in the first decade of the twentieth century – to declare that God's existence could be proved. The most classic list of proofs is that of Aquinas.

It is important to remember, however, when reading either these proofs or the millions of other Aquinas discourses, that he seldom wrote anything. He was an inspired lecturer – in Paris, in the Dominican schools of Italy and France. Although, on the shelf, Aquinas looks like the vastest, bulkiest, bookiest contrast to Socrates, who never wrote a line, he was in fact much more Socratic than, say, the philosophers of the eighteenth century who were trying to get the questions of knowledge, for instance, and how we may be said to know anything at all, all sewn up.

The eighteenth century had no difficulty in deconstructing Aquinas's ideas – developed from Aristotle – of causation: that there must be a God to have caused everything to start. But the idea is only 'theology after breakfast' if you think that Aquinas is using the word 'God' as a lazy word for 'Cause'. He never did so. For him, who, as Stevens said, 'spoke, / Kept speaking of God', the word is in fact untranslatable, and in some ways unusable.

Stevens, and modern atheism, thinks he – it – is rejecting 'religion' when he – it – rejects 'God'. In fact, nothing could be closer to orthodoxy. Nothing could be closer to the Bible.

Kierkegaard's 'God does not exist, he is eternal' would have been totally endorsed by Aquinas, as it is endorsed by the Bible.

Love requires the right 'moment'. This is as true of reading as of personal relationships. You can try to form a bond with an author at the wrong time. This happened with me and Wallace Stevens, when my daughter was at the University of Yale as a graduate student and, spending a few nights at an hotel near the green in New Haven, I had tried to read Stevens's 'An Ordinary Evening in New Haven'.

I read it over and over again and felt I was now conscious of what it must be like to have a stroke, or cerebral haemorrhage, after which, although one could hear words being spoken, they no longer quite denoted anything. I struggled to make sense, since the sentences very nearly did so, and then glided off again into a hypnotic but ultimately incomprehensible music of mere words.

> The eye's plain version is a thing apart,
> The vulgate of experience. Of this,
> A few words, an and yet, and yet, and yet—

As part of the never-ending meditation,
Part of the question that is a giant himself:
Or what is this house composed if not of the sun.

In the end, I gave up, and years were to pass before Stevens and I found our right 'moment'. By then, my daughter E. had been awarded her doctorate, moved universities, and was teaching at U. Penn. Snooty New Yorker friends expressed sympathy, either pretending that they had never been to Philadelphia, or that they had been there once for a conference or to visit some far-flung family member.

I did not see what they were talking about. The university where E. teaches, and where Ezra Pound was once (deservedly?) thrown into a pond, is a charming campus. Down in the old part of the town, there is street after street of eighteenth-century buildings. There are good art galleries and museums, and two fine rivers... And there was my beloved firstborn and her family. Good enough for me.

There can be something agitating about the demand of famous 'sights'. It was a relief, after a few visits to Philadelphia, to realize that the Liberty Bell and the various museums and galleries were, as it were, under my belt; and that in all subsequent visits, in the vacant hours, I could do what I like best in cities, which is simply wandering aimlessly. I try to do it as much as I can in London. But at home, we all scutter about, never leaving quite enough time between engagements; whereas in strange cities, there is always time to kill. When in Philadelphia, I like strolling down from Rittenhouse Square, where I generally stay, right through the Georgian part of the town, to the swift-moving Delaware, the fastest, widest river, apart from the Danube, I have ever seen. On warm days, we have sat there sketching or – when my youngest child was even younger – made expeditions over the water to the New Jersey Aquarium.

On other days, I walk beside the Schuylkill, forgetting, always, how it is pronounced, and aware, always, of how extraordinarily different it is from the Delaware: the one river seemingly possessed by might and force; the other gentle, meandering pastoral. But this day, there was no need to do anything; and, the family not expecting me for some hours, I wandered about. The walk to the river and back, which normally seems to eat time, today was accomplished double-quick. Not wanting to return to my hotel room to watch the bewildering variety of television programmes, I strolled into Barnes & Noble on Rittenhouse Square.

In the poetry section, there was L. Tall, trousered, stick thin, her dark hair now flecked a little with grey, she showed absolutely no surprise at my appearance. Though more than two years had passed since we had last met in England, it was almost as if she had made an appointment to meet me in the literature department of the bookstore.

When I think of her, in any setting, it is always holding a book very close to her face and wiggling it about, as if a light shaking would get the words into better focus. She was doing so now, with the Library of America edition of Wallace Stevens's *Collected Poetry and Prose*.

Never one for small talk, she started to recite,

> —The poem is the cry of its occasion,
> Part of the res itself and not about it.
> The poet speaks the poem as it is...

—I suppose, she said, that the deliberate appeal to Kant there is a bit clunking, but he's interesting, isn't he? I think I could get him into my Bible book.

—I tried him once and could not get on.

—Oh, I'll buy you this book. She spoke as if this would make good my deficient understanding of the poet. —You can buy me some coffee.

In those days, the presence of coffee-bars in American bookstores was a novelty for English visitors. While I fetched the foaming cups, L. was saying:

—Men, as Stevens says in the very title of one of his short poems, are 'Made out of Words'.

L. had already bought me the book. She was in mid-sentence.

—In another short poem, 'The House Was Quiet and the World Was Calm', he depicts a quiet evening in which someone is in a house, reading. Without crassly spelling out the strangeness of reading itself, the poem. . . conveys this strangeness.

> The summer night is like a perfection of thought.
> The house was quiet because it had to be.
>
> The quiet was part of the meaning, part of the mind:
> The access of perfection to the page.
>
> And the world was calm. The truth in a calm world,
> In which there is no other meaning, itself
>
> Is calm. . .

—What has that got to do with the Bible? I asked gently.

—Everything has to do with the Bible! L. laughed —Language especially. Language is always a code. Poets, the great poets, are able to wash words and make us feel they are being used for the first time. Samuel Johnson's advice – 'clear your mind of cant' – is only partially possible. To any statement, however apparently anodyne, we bring the associations of the words themselves. Naked experience, without language, is impossible, and almost all language is soaked for us in quotation, in *midrash*.

She lifted a cup to her lips as if she was about to drink, and then – a habit which had struck, and irritated, me on our very first meeting when I was aged eighteen – she put it down again, still speaking, not having drunk. (She had done exactly the same with the ginger-beer shandy in the Museum Tavern.)

—The Bible is doing two things, almost at once: it is stripping down images, and it is reaffirming images. But mainly stripping. The ban on idolatry. The making of the Golden Calf in the Wilderness. The setting up of the Golden Image by Nebuchadnezzar – all rejected. If only the people taking part in this God Debate at the moment...

—Which people?

—Some of your friends. You even wrote... she smiled... that intemperate pamphlet. You see, what I want to write about the Bible is a book which follows the three main patterns of the Book: Torah, Prophets, Writings... In its way the Bible is an experiment with language. How can you escape language, how can you live outside the mythology of language... So, although Stevens thought he was escaping the Lutheran inheritance, maybe he was in fact following it. He spent his whole life trying to write out the experience of having Lutheran ancestors, trying to unpick, or undo the rigidity of the Bible-reading forebears – whom he admired but had to escape. What he managed to do in the process of his flight was create some of the most wonderful poetry of the twentieth century.

Later in the day, I asked my daughter whether she had run into L. The question occasioned mirth.

—The tall mad-woman! She's coming to my seminar on Tragedy. She won't concentrate on the text. Last week the rest of us were trying to discuss Philoctetes, the poor man with the bleeding feet. Your friend took us on a long journey around the Book of Job, *Samson Agonistes*, the Crucifixion and Bonhoeffer – who said he could only worship a god who was a Suffering God...

I agreed with my daughter that such diversions would have put the duller students off their stride. Inwardly, however, I smiled. Attagirl.

THREE

PROPHETS

The Prophets Isaiah and Ezekiel dined with me, and I asked them
how they dared so roundly to assert that God spoke to them. . .

William Blake, *The Marriage of Heaven and Hell*

WE'D STOPPED OFF in Washington DC with H., as most
English writers of my age did if they were visiting the
American East Coast in the 1990s. He was a little older than me,
and infinitely grander in social milieu – but we had 'clicked' from the
moment we met – some ten years earlier – and he was someone of
great warmth of heart, wit and generosity. Whenever he heard that
one of his friends was coming to the East Coast, he'd urge them to
come and stay in the capital. Thoroughly assimilated as he became
as an American – I was going to write, as an American Institution,
rather than Citizen – H. was always obsessively interested in the
literary gossip of London. When we met, he would always quiz me
in detail about the staff of *The Spectator* – the magazine for which

I once worked, and at whose lunch table H. and I had first met. As well as following the doings and affairs, in all senses, of our friends there, he also had a voracious appetite for reading their work. He had always read the new novel by Peter Ackroyd or Shiva Naipaul before anyone else, and if they came to Washington, as they generally did on a book-signing tour, they would receive the same generous hospitality as R. and I were doing that evening, in a palatial apartment block once occupied by General Eisenhower, where H. and his wife and child lived like very hospitable grandees.

But on this occasion, his questions about our friends in common, and our (largely unmalicious) malice about their goings-on and their writings, were put on hold as the cigarette smoke billowed and the gin martinis were dispensed from an enormous shaker.

—So, you have taken leave of your Creator?

This was his excited question – an allusion to something I'd written back home, following on from the Jesus book, expressing total disillusionment with religion and the belief that when we looked about the world – at Northern Ireland, at the Middle East, at Sri Lanka and Burma and many of the countries in Africa – was it not religion itself, not just religious intolerance, which was causing all the trouble? This conversation took place nearly twenty years before H. himself launched into the public arena with enormously well-publicized rhetorical attacks on religion – in the form of broadcasts, lectures, brilliantly conducted public debates and books. He was to become one of the field marshals in the modern campaign against God.

I am in fact one of life's wishy-washies and, although I meant every word of my anti-religious outburst when I had written it, by the time it had appeared in print, I was beginning to have my doubts! The catechism by H. over those sublimely potent gin martinis made me feel very foolish.

—So, no reality outside ourselves – nothing Out There – no 'spiritual truth'. . .

Bushy-chested, deep-voiced – I often felt there was something Homeric about him – he began to recite the materialist creed with some fervour. I felt like some teenager who'd accidentally joined the Moonies and got in up to his neck before he'd really had time to think through the implications. H. told me gleefully that William B., a famous right-wing journalist in the US, had also recently lost his faith. He then told me an hilariously scabrous, and ludicrously camp, anecdote about the late Cardinal Spellman, Archbishop of New York.

I do not think I have ever subscribed to the hard doctrines of materialism, for the simple reason that they are based upon an almost absurdly obvious self-contradiction. In order to have reasonable discourse at all, we must be agreed that human reasoning is valid, that it can draw reasonable conclusions. 'If my mental processes are determined wholly by the motions of atoms in my brain, I have no reason to suppose that my beliefs are true. . . and hence I have no reason for supposing my brain to be composed of atoms.' If there is no order in nature, if materialism is 'all there is', if the human brain has simply evolved by a series of accidental processes, by what criterion does it come to recognize the validity or otherwise of scientific statements, or of any statements at all? In order to *know* that the material world is 'all there is', H. would have to possess a mind – which quite plainly he did. And this mind, with its capacity for ratiocination, for discourse, for turning over evidence. . . We are back to the old philosophical conundrums of consciousness being self-consciousness, of our awareness of our own minds; and back to the insoluble difference between what philosophers term Idealism versus Realism. 'By trusting to argument at all, you have assumed the point at issue', as C. S. Lewis put it, quoting J. B. S. Haldane.

But I longed to steer H. off the matter of God and his friends, and, mercifully, we left the subject eventually. Having smoked enough cigarettes to turn our lungs into kippers, and numbed the world with gin, we reeled into the dining room to eat some superb beefsteak, accompanied by flower-vase-sized goblets into which superb Château Talbot had been wastefully splashed. As the meat melted in the mouth, we at last left religion and reverted to gossip.

—We had the Duchess through last week signing her latest.

—Debo?

—Madama Ackroyd.

R. and I left DC the next morning for Charleston. My wife was even more anxious than I was to see the antebellum architectural treasures, and my publisher, S., had a house adjoining a country club a few miles from the city. Over dinner we told him about our time in DC, met some of his family, of whom I was growing fond, and talked about our sightseeing plans.

—That all sounds great, he said. —But tomorrow is Martin Luther King Day, and I'd like to drive over to this place called the Penn Center. It's on one of the Sea Islands. Dr King often went there for retreats, and to preach, and. . . well, if you'd care to come along. . .

It was a longer drive than I'd expected, and it was dark before we got to the Penn Center. The hall – if my memory serves me right, it wasn't a chapel, exactly – was completely packed, and we were welcomed effusively. We were not quite the only whites in the place, but it felt like that. I felt stiff with shyness. Although – almost, because – the people at the door were so friendly, did they think we had just come as spectators, not participants, in what was to follow?

There was a large gospel choir assembled, and before long the music began. This was the first time in my life that I had heard this music. It was an intoxicant, and as with the effects of alcohol, muscles relaxed and the mind moved more freely. A good gospel song starts with a slow recitative – sometimes the personal testimony of a soloist, sometimes a few lines sung in chorus. Then the rhythm starts to establish itself. Then the song moves into top gear, a lively hymn of praise. It was during the singing of 'The Blood Done Signed My Name' that I really gave myself up to the music... Lead me, dear Master, to ma home above... The Blood will never lose its Power...

Surely no one, except the totally cloth-eared, can hear that music without hearing two centuries and more of dignified human suffering, two centuries and more in which African people had been treated like chattels, kidnapped, exiled, forced into punitively hard labour and enslaved. Almost the most painful part of the story is what happened after they were supposedly 'liberated' and slavery was abolished, but still, especially in the Southern States, the vast majority of African Americans lived in abject poverty and were exposed to the most degrading discrimination.

Perhaps those of a generation younger than I am – I was born in 1950 – find it hard to envisage a world in which one category of human beings, in the free, democratic United States, were allowed into certain schools, toilets, buses, from which other categories of person were excluded. And perhaps no one who has lived in latter times can quite recapture how exciting it was to live in a world which contained Dr Martin Luther King, nor how the Civil Rights Movement, and the anti-Vietnam war movement, came to a tragic crescendo in 1968 with the assassination of King, and of Bobby Kennedy.

As the voices swelled – I Rose up this Mornin' with the Holy Ghost – I began to envisage Dr King himself standing in that quite small hall and addressing his followers. I have only ever heard him deliver his famous speeches on film. Whether preaching from the pulpit or delivering a political message from the podium, his rhetoric follows a pattern which is in fact very similar to that of the gospel song. He would start, in his modulated and very educated tone, to expound his theme. If he was preaching from the Bible, he would usually make it clear that he had read the relevant modern commentaries on the Scriptural passage and took a non-fundamentalist view of the text. He would then draw out its poetry. To this extent, he was most perfectly true to the tradition of Christian Scripture reading which we find in Paul's Epistles, in Hebrews, and in the early Fathers of the Church – expounding the 'literal' reading of a text, and then moving towards an exposition of its 'true' meaning.

As he did so, his voice and manner would change. He would move, as it were, from the 'recitative' to the rhythmic chorus, often repeating a phrase over and over again – as in the most famous of all his speeches – 'I Have a Dream'. And the larynx would then become vibrato, and he would move to his peroration.

It is difficult to think of anyone in my lifetime (I was born after the death of Gandhi) who more deserves the name of prophet than

Dr King. Nor is it easy to think of any figure who was more Biblical. One thinks of his sermon delivered, I think, at Atlanta, Georgia, on the three young men, Shadrach, Meshach and Abednego, in the Book of Daniel, who refused to bow down and worship the image set up by King Nebuchadnezzar. The title and text of the sermon was 'But if Not!'

As the sober Harvard Ph.D. expositor of the original text in Daniel moved into choric mode, the simple Bible story began to be applied to the current situation in the American South. Even if the demonstrations and the boycotts and the protests got apparently nowhere, they were still going to continue – because it was right to protest and because, eventually, he had confidence that they would succeed.

His extraordinary speech in Memphis on the eve of his assassination foresaw that, like Moses, who died on Mount Nebo before he was able to get to Canaan, he would never enter the Land of Promise. King saw political and social events in the light of the Bible, and deliberately used the language and lore of the Bible to speak of his campaign for Civil Rights. Reared in the African-American Baptist tradition, he absorbed the 'modern' approaches to the Bible text, studying the German critics and theologians. Early in his ministry, however, he abandoned the arid textual methods of the twentieth-century Germans and reverted to a much older way of reading the Bible – using allegory and typology as methods of interpreting the old stories, just as Augustine and the early Fathers of the Church had done. He did not need to teach this way of reading the Bible to his congregations – they already read it that way themselves, seeing their own struggles and dilemmas reflected in the story of Moses delivering the enslaved people of Israel from

Egypt to the Promised Land. While academics all over the Western world were letting the Bible turn into a dead letter beneath their imperceptive scrutiny, King and his followers found it to be a living Word which inspired them to live and to act and to become free:

> My soul is sick, my heart is sore
> Now I'm coming home
> My strength renew, my hope restore
> Lord, I'm coming home.

His rhetoric was consciously Biblical, and the more practically political he became, the more he invoked the Bible, uttering speeches which had Hebrew parallelism in their poetry.

> If we are wrong, the Supreme Court of this nation is wrong. If we are wrong, the Constitution of the United States is wrong. If we are wrong, God Almighty is wrong. If we are wrong, Jesus of Nazareth was merely a utopian dreamer that never came down to Earth. If we are wrong, justice is a lie, love has no meaning. And we are determined here in Montgomery to work and fight until justice runs down like water and righteousness like a mighty stream.

The metaphor of the 'Dream' speech is as old as the prophet Joel's visions – 'your old men shall dream dreams, and your young men shall see visions.' [Joel 2:28]

King's sermons all have the vividness of poetry:

You *can't* hem him [mankind] in.
He has a mind.
Hold John Bunyan
In Bedford *jail*
He set there
But because he had a *mind*
His mind leaped out of the bars.

Using Christ's parable of Dives and Lazarus, King compared Africa to a beggar lying at Europe's doorstep. Before a march in Albany, he declared:

We will march around
Those jail house walls
That symbolize segregation
We will walk around them
Like unto Joshua
Until the walls
Come tumblin' down.

The academic world was taken over, during the 1970s, by what was called Theory, sometimes Critical Theory. One of its cardinal doctrines was that expressed by, among others, the Canadian theorist Jean-François Lyotard who spoke of 'the end of grand narratives' (in *The Postmodern Condition*). The grand narrative is one which encompasses all others. Lyotard – deriving from Derrida and other theorists – wanted to make his devotees believe that 'grand narrative' was either sinister – as it had been in the time of the National Socialists

– or simply fallacious. Yet the template of all templates, the Grand Narrative of all Grand Narratives in the West, has been the Bible; and only a few years before Critical Theory swept the campuses, King had demonstrated the power of the Grand Narrative.

I suppose a secularist like my friend H. in Washington would have said that the important thing about King was that he began a tide of demonstration against an unquestionable evil, that as well as possessing the gift of oratory he had prodigious organizational skills. The bus boycott in Atlanta was only the beginning. In the final Memphis speech, he had calculated that, though the American blacks were poor, their collective income exceeded the GDP of Canada. When he began to tell them not to buy Coca-Cola or not to invest in white-run insurance companies, he was wielding some mighty economic clout.

It was this, the secularist H. would have argued, and not the guff about the Book of Daniel, which gave King his power and his place in the history books. But if this *is* what he thought (and I am putting words in his mouth), this is so facile, and so wrong!

H. had wanted me to agree that not only was 'religion' all rubbish; but it was also a form of mental poison, responsible for so many of the pointless conflicts in the world. I'd nodded in agreement as the martinis made a Cloud of Unknowing in my skull, but here was a glaring example of a phenomenon which was the opposite of mental poison.

African Americans, through their spirituals, through their Baptist and other chapels, through their traditions of song, carried around with them, from their first arrival as slaves until the present day, a collective way of reading the Bible.

They knew that a 'fundamentalist' or 'literalist' view of Scripture justifies slavery, rather than the reverse. Both the Old and the New Testaments were written during periods when slaves were a fact of life, and you could even justify, as the right-wing whites in South Africa could do for many years, the oppression of black people by whites from the story of Ham (father of Cain) gazing on his father Noah's nakedness and being punished. 'Lowest of slaves shall he be to his brothers.' [Genesis 9:25] But the American slaves and their descendants were not Biblical literalists. They were People of the Book.

Rather than using the Bible as a weapon with which to strike their enemies, they saw it as filled with symbolic and collective significance. Their instantaneous identification with the enslaved Hebrews in Egypt, for example, was not a fanciful reading of the Torah. It was the authentic way of reading it. The ones who have got that story wrong include the academics who insist that the whole story of Moses is 'myth' and therefore of no value to the historian; and the fundamentalists who think that these rich stories somehow or other justify the drawing-up of certain territorial borderlines in the twenty-first-century Gaza or West Bank. Those are the strangely linked fundamentalists who get the Bible wrong. But the slaves who sang 'Go Down Moses' and the oppressed African Americans who joined the Civil Rights Movement, and Dr King, they are the ones who knew How to Read the Bible. They remake it the Book of the People.

∝⟩

After Samuel had anointed Saul, and proclaimed him the King of Israel, the old priest told him that, as he came down the road to Gibeath-Elohim, 'at the place where the Philistine garrison is; there, as you come into the town, you will meet a band of prophet coming down from the shrine with harp, tambourine, flute, and lyre playing in front of them; they will be in a prophetic frenzy. Then the spirit of the Lord will possess you and you will be in a prophetic frenzy along with them and be turned into a different person. Now when these signs meet you, do whatever you see fit to do, for God is with you.' [I Samuel 10:5–7]

The root meaning of 'to prophesy' is probably a verb meaning 'to slaver', 'to foam at the mouth'. As Martin Luther King's biographer Richard Lischer wrote, 'Hebrew scholars contend that prophets are "maladjusted" figures whose "pathological" visions are given utterances in tones "one octave too high for our ears".'

Some Bible scholars believe that the prophetic tradition stretches right back, a thousand years BC. The first prophets whose words and actions are recorded in books of the Bible emerged in the eighth century BC. Amos is the earliest – he was active during the peaceful reign of Jeroboam II, 788–747 BC. Amos was a sheep-farmer in the southern Kingdom of Judah. Moved by the Spirit of the Lord, he began to denounce the religious hypocrisy, and the social injustices, of the northern kingdom, Israel. The key sentence in the entire book – one beloved of Dr King himself – was 'The Lord God has spoken; who can but prophesy?' [Amos 3:8]

Although Amos uttered his prophecies at a period when monotheism was very far from being established, he was a monotheist of sorts. Two things distinguish his powerful utterances.

The first is his sense of the Lord being the Lord of all – who made the earth and the stars and the world of men and women: 'The one who made the Pleiades and Orion, and turns deep darkness into the morning, and darkens the day into night, who calls for the waters of the sea, and pours them out on the surface of the earth, the Lord is his name' [Amos 5:8].

Second, Amos, who spoke in the name of the Lord God, is convinced that God communicates via the human conscience. We know the difference between right and wrong, and in making these discernments, we come to know God. 'For lo, the one who forms the mountain, creates the wind, reveals his thoughts to mortals, makes the morning darkness, and treads on the heights of the earth – the Lord, the God of hosts, is his name!' [Amos 4:13] In the later prophecies of Ezekiel, a Temple priest who was taken into exile in Babylon in 597 BC with the first tranche of Hebrew exiles, there is a vivid metaphor: 'A new heart I will give you, and a new spirit I will put within you; and I will remove from your body the heart of stone and give you a heart of flesh. I will put my spirit within you, and make you follow my statutes and be careful to observe my ordinances.' [Ezekiel 36:26–27]

But the Hebrew prophets did not preach a merely private religion. True, they called every man, woman and child to pray for that new heart of flesh, in place of the heart of stone. True, they preached personal repentance. But they were also passionately engaged with a quest for social justice. They were not monks or contemplatives. Their possessed, or frenzied, utterances were commentaries on actual world events, and they called for the all-out reform of the system. That is why a figure such as Amos, the small sheep-farmer who took on the kings and rulers, denouncing their greed and selfishness and neglect of the poor, was so inspiring to Martin Luther King.

There are many prophets in the Hebrew Bible, but the archetypical prophet was Elijah, whose story is told in the First Book of Kings. His clashes with the evil King Ahab and with the pagan, self-indulgent Queen Jezebel in the Kingdom of Israel make up some of the most memorable narratives in the whole of Scripture.

When the prophet encountered the king, Ahab, in his greeting, gave the definition of a prophet in the Biblical tradition: "'Is it you, you troubler of Israel?" He answered, "I have not troubled Israel; but you have, and your father's house, because you have forsaken the commandments of the Lord and followed the Baals.'" [1 Kings 18:17–18] There followed a vast assembly on Mount Carmel, where Elijah challenged the four hundred and fifty pagan prophets (prophets of Baal) to a competition. He told the crowds who assembled that they must choose between following the popular pagan religion promulgated by Queen Jezebel and her false prophets, or following Yahweh, the true God. "'I, even I only, am left a prophet of the Lord; but Baal's prophets number four hundred fifty.'" [1 Kings 18:22]

Two bulls were brought. Elijah took one of the animals, and the priests of Baal another. The competition was to see which God – the Lord or Baal – would set light to a burnt offering merely by prayer, without the fire being lit by human hand. From morning to noon, the prophets of Baal limped around their altar offering their imprecations to Baal, and as they did so, Elijah mocked them: "'Cry aloud! Surely he is a god; either he is meditating, or he has wandered away, or he is on a journey, or perhaps he is asleep and must be awakened.'" [1 Kings 18:27]

Here is a classic exposition of how the Torah, the Prophets and the Wisdom Literature of the Bible all spell out the same 'atheist' message. Our contemporary denouncers of theism and religion are nearly always operating, though they would not recognize this, in the tradition of Elijah's speech on Mount Carmel. The true God cannot be destroyed by human satire or human attempts at logic. He is God! But the lazy substitutes for science or substitutes for logic which masquerade as theology or religion – these are rightly destroyed by the arguments of H. and his friends.

After the prophets of Baal had been reduced to despair, cutting themselves with swords and lances as they cried out to their non-existent god Baal, it was the turn of Elijah. He cut up his bull and laid it on the altar. Then he asked the helpers to dig a trench around the altar and filled it with water. Again. And again. Having doused his meat and stones with water, Elijah called upon the name of the Lord, 'God of Abraham, Isaac and Israel' [1 Kings 18:36].

Fire came from heaven. Elijah was vindicated. He took all four hundred and fifty false prophets to the Wadi Kishon and slaughtered them.

It is not a gentle tale! But nor does it end there. Having proved his case, and slaughtered the false prophets, Elijah's life was in grave danger from Jezebel. He went into hiding, in a cave on Mount Horeb, and there he sank into a profound depression.

> Then the word of the Lord came to him, saying, 'What are you doing here, Elijah?' He answered, 'I have been very zealous for the Lord, the God of hosts; for the Israelites have forsaken your covenant, thrown down your altars, and killed

your prophets with the sword. I alone am left, and they are seeking my life, to take it away.'

He said, 'Go out and stand on the mountain before the Lord, for the Lord is about to pass by.' Now there was a great wind, so strong that it was splitting mountains and breaking rocks in pieces before the Lord, but the Lord was not in the wind; and after the wind an earthquake, but the Lord was not in the earthquake; and after the earthquake a fire, but the Lord was not in the fire; and after the fire a sound of sheer silence. [1 Kings 19:9–12]

It is in the 'still small voice of calm' that the prophet hears the voice of the true God.

After the Babylonian exile, the Biblical writers conveyed a sense that the voice of prophecy ceased. In Psalm 74, for instance, the writer asks God, 'why do you cast us off forever?' As the poet imagines their enemy destroying the sanctuary and hacking at the adorned Temple with hatchets and hammers – it was a Psalm which Dietrich Bonhoeffer marked in his prayer book with the date of Kristallnacht – he states, 'We do not see our emblems; there is no longer any prophet' [Psalm 74:9].

The rabbinic literature believed that, just as the kings of Israel and Judah died out, so did the prophets. 'After the first temple was destroyed, kingship ceased from the house of David, the Urim and the Thummim ceased... After Haggai, Zechariah and Malachi – the latter prophets died – the Holy Spirit departed from Israel.'

It was at this moment that the Jews felt the need for Scripture, and began either to write the books we now call the Bible, or to compile older writings into the shape they came to possess as Biblical texts. Whether you take the view that the Bible texts were written in the fourth to second centuries BC, or whether you follow another strand of modern scholarship and believe that the Bible is actually much older – largely written between the reigns of King Hezekiah (r.715–687 BC) and King Josiah (r.640–609 BC) – does not really alter the argument here.

Plato recorded the sayings and conversations of his hero Socrates, and there was something deeply paradoxical about this exercise. For Socrates made it clear that we arrive at the truth by the oral examination of concepts and ideas, by talk, by conversational to and fro. To freeze such concepts into written dialogues, highly elaborate written constructs, is of course to change their nature entirely. And Socrates, incidentally, rather like the oral prophets of old Israel, was believed to be possessed by a particular Spirit.

Likewise, the spoken words of inspired prophets differ markedly from written words. This is not just because the scribe who wrote them might have distorted the words, like the idiotic evangelist in Bulgakov's *The Master and Margarita*, who keeps misquoting the Master. It is because the spoken word is living, and the written word cannot live in the same way. Not all the Biblical authors would have agreed with Paul, writing to his Christian converts in Corinth that 'the letter kills, but the Spirit gives life' [2 Corinthians3:6], but the prophets, and Socrates, would have seen the point when he told his followers, 'You yourselves are our letter, written on our hearts, to be known and read by all' [2 Corinthians 3:2].

Judaism is so intensely literate a religion, based not just on written Biblical texts, but on the written commentaries made by the rabbis on those texts, and then further commentaries on the commentaries, that we can be forgiven for not distinguishing the world where the Bible originated from its later life in the rabbinic schools and the synagogues.

The legendary happenings of the Bible (the Fall of Man, Noah, the Hebrew Enslavement in Egypt, the Journey through the Wilderness, and so on) happened not merely in times which, if not prehistoric in the palaeolithic sense, are pre-realist history. But they are also pre-writing. The alphabet came into general use in the world at about the time of the first world empire, the Assyrian, in the eighth century BC, which was also the time of the first written prophecies in Hebrew. In this world, literacy was not just rare, it was all but non-existent for most people.

In the pre-history times – pre-history, that is, as far as the Bible is concerned, in the second millennium BC – writing, pre-alphabetic writing, was always sacred. It was a sacred or magical act. Among the earliest forms of writing to be found are inscriptions on or near Egyptian coffins from the third millennium BC. Their magical rituals reflect the idea that writing could actually spring to life, possess a magical life of its own. It is to this 'pre-historic' mode of writing that the Ten Commandments belong when God's Finger actually traced the Torah on stone for Moses [Exodus 24:12].

Once we enter the era where the Bible becomes history, the written word, and our attitude to it, begins to change. After this, there can exist the illusion that the inspired or spoken word is really more lively than the inscribed or written word. Two things seem to happen at once here. On the one hand, the written – still more the engraved – word has authority. It conveys, and reflects, power. Write something down and we are beginning to move towards a time when it is unchangeable. On the other hand, while all these texts were preserved by writing and reading, there remain, in a number of literate traditions, the illusions of orality. Plato, one of the greatest *writers* of the ancient world, managed to make a hero out of a man who never wrote a word, Socrates. What are in fact carefully crafted literary texts, written by Plato, come to us as the oral effusions of Socrates. In a comparable way, 'orality was… an ideology of Rabbinic Judaism'. The Rabbis believed that the spoken Torah had more authority than the written Torah. But this is going to lead us round and round in circles; because, of course, the writing down of spontaneous utterance is the only way they possessed of immortalizing it.

This duality, this tension between the 'inspired' Word of God and the sacred quality of the Written, is something which the Bible brings down through history, packed into each of its books. It explains many of the spats, in Judaism and Christianity, between the 'prophetic' or 'ecstatic' interpreters of the Word and those who believe in a sacred and unalterable Text.

The Biblical tradition of the prophets brings this out very clearly. The Bible is calling us to tear out our hearts of stone and replace them with hearts of flesh. That is why so many of the prophets of the twentieth century were inspired, as was Dr King, by the Biblical spirit of prophecy, which in Christianity is developed into the notion of God's Word, not merely spoken, but incarnated, made flesh. Although the Word was only made flesh once in the formal doctrinal sense, there is another sense in which the Word is made flesh, in Biblical terms, every time the prophetic spirit is invoked, every time the hunger for justice is fulfilled.

It was late when we returned to the country club from the Penn Center.

—I forgot, said S. —Someone wrote to you and posted it to my office in New York. Here—

He held out an envelope, inscribed with the familiar italic of L.

Seeing the postmark, he asked,

—Who d'you know in Kentucky?

—No one.

What was she doing there? Buying a horse?

> Trying to get to grips with the chapter on the Prophets for How to Read the Bible.

I did not recognize the name of the place at the time. L. was staying in the guest house at the Abbey of Gethsemani, the Trappist monastery where Thomas Merton had pursued his pilgrimage. She did not directly allude to my tirade 'against religion', but presumably she meant some reference to it when she wrote:

> So much of the anti-religious feeling in the West seems to be a form of laziness: not bothering to listen to what our ancestors were saying: not having any use for the old furniture and pictures inherited by our grandparents, so chucking them all out. Previous generations have been enlivened by the Bible,

not held back by it, because they have always been able to read it as a template of how their own lives – as individual and as groups – are to be led: the Abolitionists, for example, who campaigned for the scrapping of slavery, were all guided by the Bible in one way or another, just as the slaves were all sustained by their ability to transpose their own situation on to the stories of the Hebrew slaves in Egypt, and their journey through the desert to the freedom of the Promised Land. I think I want to write about this in my chapter on the Prophets...

When Jesus was Transfigured – when he appeared to be shining with light on the mountain and his three friends saw him conversing with Moses and Elijah – how did they know it was Moses and Elijah?!! No one had ever taken photographs of these individuals.

Yet it is one of the most popular scenes for Icons in the Eastern Church. We are to take it that in this moment he was shown to be the fulfilment of two strands of Jewish tradition – the Torah, in Moses, and the Prophetic tradition. It was his life as a prophet, denouncing the wrongdoing of his day, that led him to the Cross.

On the plane coming over, I read a life of Trevor Huddleston, the Anglican bishop who did so much to campaign against apartheid twenty years ago in South Africa and got expelled for his pains. He said in one of his sermons, 'The Christian, if he is true to his calling, is always an agitator... At the heart of our religion there lies a principle in absolute contradiction to the principles by which the world speaks and thinks and acts.'

While King and his followers campaigned for justice in the United States, in South Africa a parallel struggle was advancing against apartheid, spearheaded by some Anglican monks, the two most prominent of whom were Raymond Raynes and Trevor Huddleston. When I wrote to L. about the experience of hearing the gospel singers at the Penn Center, she sent back another quotation from one of Huddleston's Christmas sermons in South Africa: 'It is this mystery of identification which finds its expression in the Stable of Bethlehem – God Almighty and Eternal, identifying Himself with man at his most helpless, with man in his utter littleness and poverty. Surely if the Incarnation means anything at all, it must mean the breaking down of barriers not by words, but by deeds, by acts, by identification.'

She added:

> The Word, in other words, is always two things, which is what is meant by its taking Flesh. The Word is active (King, Huddleston, any prophetic engagement with the world, whether in the Civil Rights Movement, Oxfam, the anti-apartheid movement, etc., etc.) and it is also written. Words are not just spoken. Socrates to this extent is a fictional character. And the Jesus of the Gospels??? Fascinating that Solzhenitsyn was beginning his painstaking dedication to the Word – writing out the experiences of his fellow-prisoners in the Gulag Archipelago, as these other heroes (roughly) were fighting for truth and justice in the American South and in South Africa...

It is indeed a strange fact that at the very same period in history that Dr King was leading his followers to Mount Nebo and showing them the Promised Land of an end to segregation, an end to discrimination, an end to the iniquity of racism in the United States, an obscure physics teacher from Rostov in the Soviet Union was writing his own commentary on the Scriptures in the form of *One Day in the Life of Ivan Denisovich* and had already begun his furious exposé of the Gulag Archipelago.

When I was in my twenties, in the 1970s, if you had asked anyone in Western Europe or the United States to name a celebrated author, they would almost certainly have said Alexander Solzhenitsyn. Yet now his memory has vanished almost without trace.

Extraordinary.

In *One Day in the Life of Ivan Denisovich*, Alyosha, the Baptist in a neighbouring bunk, had copied out half the New Testament into a notebook which he kept concealed in a crack in the wall, invisible to the warders. He read from it aloud so that Ivan D. can hear:

> The Baptist was reading his Bible, not altogether silently, but sort of sighing out the words. This was meant perhaps for Shukhov. (A bit like political agitators, these Baptists. Loved spreading the word.)
>
> 'But let none of you suffer as a murderer, or a thief, or a wrongdoer, or a mischief-maker; yet if one suffers as a Christian, let him not be ashamed, but under that name let him glorify God.'

These are all ways of reading the Bible.

☙

The folkloric books of Samuel and Kings were included in the synagogue libraries in the section reserved for Prophecies. Although they contain some of the most famous stories in the world – the boy David fighting the giant Goliath, the ravens feeding the prophet Elijah, King Solomon, the wisest man in the world, being visited by the Queen of Sheba – they are fundamentally imbued with a single prophetic message. That message is that Israel, and later Judah, made a fundamental mistake in asking God to give them a human king. God was, and is, their King.

In 1 Samuel 8, the people approach their old prophetic patriarch, Samuel, with the request: "'You are old and your sons do not follow in your ways; appoint for us, then, a king to govern us, like other nations.'" [1 Samuel 8:5] Samuel consulted God, who said, "'Listen to the voice of the people. . . for they have not rejected you, but they have rejected me from being king over them.'" [1 Samuel 8:7]

Samuel warned the people against monarchy.

> These will be the ways of the king who will reign over you: he will take your sons and appoint them to his chariots and to be his horsemen, and to run before his chariots; and he will appoint for himself commanders of thousands and commanders of fifties, and some to plow his ground and to reap his harvest, and to make his implements of war and the equipment of his chariots. He will take your daughters to be perfumers and cooks and bakers. He will take the best of

your fields and vineyards and olive orchards and give them to
his courtiers. [1 Samuel 8:10–15]

Embedded in the prophetic tradition is the everlastingly revolutionary idea that God never wanted his people to have a king, and
nor did he want them to have a temple. That is why, in history,
those who hate throne and altar, whether Milton or Voltaire, have
something recognizably of the Divine Spark.

Jesus stood before Pilate, having been mockingly crowned with
thorns. He recognized the authority of Caesar, but reverted to the
true prophetic ideal of Israel when he said, 'Give to the emperor the
things that are the emperor's, and to God the things that are God's.'
[Mark 12:17]

Solzhenitsyn's prophetic witness could not take the oral,
and dramatic, form of the Civil Rights Movement in America.
Imprisoned for years in the Gulag Archipelago, in common with
millions of others, he knew that vocalized dissent would have led to
instant death. It must often have been an extinction for which each
and every prisoner of the Stalinist regime yearned. But Alexander
Solzhenitsyn wanted the world to know what was happening
behind the impassive cruel façade of Soviet communism. Now,
forty years later, we all know what was happening and we can read
such magisterial surveys as those of the Pulitzer prize-winning
Anne Applebaum's *Gulag: A History*. But when Solzhenitsyn's
work began to appear in the West, it was a revelation. We knew
that Stalin had been cruel, we knew he employed secret police, we
knew that many millions had died in the civil war, in the purges, in
the Second World War. The extent of the enslavement, the sheer

numbers of dissidents killed or imprisoned, however, we did not know. The sheer magnitude of the Stalinist propaganda lie we did not know. And the first major work of demolition was that of Solzhenitsyn.

After his exile in Vermont, and his subsequent return to a post-Soviet Russia, Solzhenitsyn excited much controversy, not least for his defence, in the second volume of *The Gulag Archipelago*, of those thousands of Russian troops, at the end of the Second World War, who had been prepared to side with the Germans in an attempt to destroy the Stalinist tyranny.

These are matters of controversy which will never go away, but they should not be allowed to diminish his stature. Here was one who held the emperor to account, and who in so doing, during the long years in prison, came to share the Christian faith which he had first seen among the Baptists and later rediscovered in his own Orthodox Church.

What he has in common with Civil Rights campaigners, and with the anti-apartheid campaigners, is a Biblical sense of prophecy. Those who regard religion as mental poison blind themselves to the forcefulness of religion as a power for good against monstrous injustices. All over Eastern Europe, partly inspired by Solzhenitsyn, partly inspired by the leadership of the Archbishop of Cracow, later Pope John Paul II, men and women rejected Marxist Materialism and the brutal system which it had inflicted upon them. The religion of the Scriptures, the Christian religion, was not just a cultural adjunct to their struggle: it was the fundamental inspiration. Christ stood before Pilate, and the world saw that the spirit of prophecy was not dead.

FOUR

HOLY WISDOM

There was a muddy centre before we breathed.
There was a myth before the myth began,
Venerable and articulate and complete.

Wallace Stevens, 'Notes Toward a Supreme Fiction',
Part I: 'It Must Be Abstract'

I F YOU ARE old-fashioned enough to be reading this in book-form, you are holding a codex. Even if you are reading this electronically, the device on which the page appears nonetheless imitates the codex – that is, the sort of book where you turn pages. That is the form in which most of us have read the Bible, though we might have attended services at a synagogue in which the revered Jewish Law, the Torah, was carried about to glorious chants in its scrolls, texts which are so venerated that they are often encased in exquisite containers.

For a Jew, the Torah is the Law of God. It is a word which we translate as Law, and which also refers to the first five books in the

Bible – sometimes called the Books of Moses. Many Jews would think it strange that I am writing a book about the Bible and concentrating not on the Torah, but on Wisdom.

If you'd opened the bookshelves in an old synagogue, before the codex was invented, and long before there was a Christian Bible, you would have found they had arranged the scrolls in three sections. Indeed, the very word given by Jews for their Hebrew Bible is an acronym of these three sections: Tanakh – standing for Torah (the Law), Nevi'im (the Prophets) and Kethuvim (the Writings). First, the Torah, the Books of Moses. These were the works which were recited all the time. Another shelf would be reserved for the Prophets (Nevi'im). These scrolls would contain not only the three major prophets – Isaiah, Jeremiah and Ezekiel – and the twelve minor ones, but also the works we know as histories – Joshua, Judges and the two double books of Samuel and Kings. These 'Prophets' would only have been read very selectively, some of them hardly at all.

There was a third section, known as the Writings, or simply as the Scrolls. These would contain the Psalms, which were well known and often used as the hymnbook of the synagogue, but also the parts of the Bible sometimes referred to as the Wisdom Literature. Some of these writings are very ancient. The Book of Job, for example, dates probably from the sixth or late fifth century BC. Other parts of Wisdom Literature, especially some of those books which were not included in the finished canon of the Hebrew Bible, such as 'The Wisdom of Solomon', possibly dates from as early as 100 BC, but could be later.

The cult of 'Wisdom' in the period when this book was composed grew up in parts of Jewry which had been Hellenized. In 'The

Wisdom of Solomon' the worship of 'Lady Wisdom' bears analogy with Greek prose poems celebrating the Egyptian goddess Isis, the patron of Wisdom. The pursuit of Wisdom, the worship of Wisdom, the personification of Wisdom as a beautiful lady, are all central to this book, but also to a particular way of reading the Bible.

Let us leap ahead half a millennium, after the composition of 'The Wisdom of Solomon', to the point where Europe meets Asia, the high promontory which juts out above the Bosphorus and looks towards the Sea of Marmara, where Jason once sailed with the Argonauts.

It is one of the most stunning places in the world. A city was here in pre-Roman times, named Byzantium, but it was only with the decline of Rome, and the decision of the Emperor Constantine to rebuild this Rome of the East as Constantinople, that the origins of the modern city were founded. It was here, in the beginning of the sixth century, that the Emperor Justinian built his astounding church, dedicated to Holy Wisdom – Hagia Sophia in Greek, Aya Sofya in modern Turkish.

It was for many centuries the largest building in the world. Its huge dome was an architectural miracle. Procopius, the Greek historian who wrote in the middle of the sixth century, said that 'whenever one enters the church to pray, one understands immediately that it has been fashioned not by any human power or skill but by the influence of God. And so the mind is lifted up to God.' When the Russian Prince Vladimir of Kiev attended the liturgy in this place, he recorded that 'we knew not whether we were in heaven or on earth. For on earth there is no such splendour or such beauty, and we are at a loss how to describe it.'

In the century after the Council of Chalcedon in 451, the Divine Liturgy of the Church underwent many embellishments and changes, including a newly composed Communion chant which would have been performed with unmatched pomp in this building; and, on the annual celebration of the Lord's Supper on Maundy Thursday, after the Bread and Wine had been transformed by the Holy Spirit into the Body and Blood of Christ, the choir now sang, 'At your mystical supper, Son of God, receive me today as a partaker, for I will not betray the sacrament to your enemies, nor give you a kiss like Judas, but like the thief I confess you: remember me, Lord, in your kingdom.' There could be few more vivid illustrations of the way in which building and liturgy grow organically out of Scripture.

The great church, with its huge spaces, was once encrusted with gold mosaics, only very few of which survive. It suffered dreadful spoliation from the oafish, vandalistic soldiers who arrived from Western Europe on the Fourth Crusade, and in 1453, after the conquest of the city by Muslims, it was not long before it lost its status as a church. The covering up of the mosaics, the stripping of the interior splendours, the addition of carpets, all did much to diminish the glory of the building, and the hanging of huge Islamic calligraphic discs at each corner of the dome prevented the eye soaring, and the mind dreaming. These texts announced that the People of the Book had arrived, and the church, one of the finest creations inspired by the Book of the People, sat uneasily beneath its Islamic manifestation. The subsequent addition of minarets outside is an interruption to the building's domed outline.

When Turkey was defeated in the First World War, Lord Curzon, the British Foreign Secretary, wanted Hagia Sophia to be reconverted to a Christian church. I wonder if he hoped, in the process, to bring it into line with the Church of England. The dream of hearing Stanford's *Magnificat in C* echo through those vast spaces and waft upwards to the enormous dome, was never realized. In the early 1930s, in accordance with Ataturk's secularization of Turkey, the mosque itself became a museum. Such is its status to this day. In order to see it in anything approaching peace, you must be first through the door in the morning, before the tourists arrive in their thousands. Such is the size and splendour of the building, however, that it is still possible for it to speak to us, though with less eloquence than when it so bowled over the Byzantine worshippers of the past, and the Russian visitors whom it converted to Orthodoxy.

Many years had passed since my visit to Nablus with R. We had been married a long time. We had a twelve-year-old child. Visiting Istanbul for a week, we had devised the perfect means of passing the day. Because I wake early, I sat on the roof of the small hotel, reading Gibbon's *Decline and Fall of the Roman Empire*, when there was still cool in the air. Behind the hotel, the immense dome of Hagia Sophia was seen against the blue sky. Ahead, shimmering in morning mist, was the Sea of Marmara. After breakfast, there was sightseeing. And then, when the heat of the day began to get up, we would go down to the docks at the Adalar terminal in Kabataş, and take one of the regular ferry-boats out to the Princes' Islands, for an afternoon of swimming.

Hagia Sophia can only be partially imagined from photographs. It is a spatial wonder. Even after the first busloads have disgorged their hundreds, you can find peace in the vast galleries, where patient restorers have managed to uncover some of the most glorious mosaics you will see anywhere in the world. And from the marbled galleries, it is almost possible to imagine the elaborate ceremonials which went on there for the first nine hundred years of its existence. Nine hundred years is a very long time, and the numbers of worshippers in that space of time must be counted in the millions. If we listen to them, they are telling us something of central importance about the Bible. And when we come down from the gallery and stand in the South Porch, looking up at the beautiful mosaic of Justinian, Constantine and the Mother of God, we understand why the Church is dedicated to Holy Wisdom. We understand, moreover, the whole starting point of the Christian Bible, and of the Christian view of the world.

The church was dedicated on Christmas Day, 538, and this mosaic tells us why.

To our left, the Emperor Justinian is offering his church to the Mother of God. The dolls'-house-sized version of the great church which he holds in his hands is clearly recognizable as the mighty domed structure we see today. To our right the Emperor Constantine is offering the Mother of God the city itself. Here we see the whole of Byzantine civilization, from Constantine to Justinian, from the fourth to the sixth century, dedicating itself to Mary and her Child.

Why to them, and why on Christmas Day? Because the Holy Wisdom, or the Word of God, interchangeable terms in the Greek version of the Scriptures, became flesh on Christmas Day. Holy Wisdom is another word for Jesus.

The Church of the Holy Wisdom in Istanbul is one of the great readings of the Bible. It would not exist had there not been a particular telling and retelling, working and reworking of Biblical texts. We think that our way of presenting narratives, through 'straight' reportage, through linear and apparently dispassionate chronicling of 'facts', is the only way of telling a story. But the Church of the Holy Wisdom, and the Bible which enshrines an idea of Holy Wisdom, teaches otherwise.

The Holy Wisdom, or the Christ, of God were there first, as concepts. It was these concepts of which the New Testament writers availed themselves when speaking of Jesus.

In the Greek Bible, in the twenty-fourth chapter of the Book of Sirach, there is an exquisite poem in which Wisdom, a female personification, speaks. She says that she came forth out of the mouth of God and covered the earth like a mist [Sirach 24:3]. She speaks of herself, whose dwelling was heaven, seeking a place to live on earth: 'Then the Creator of all things gave me a command, and my Creator chose the place for my tent. He said, "Make your dwelling in Jacob, and in Israel receive your inheritance".' [Sirach 24:8]

The book was probably first written in Hebrew in Jerusalem some time in 180 BC. It would seem to have been written by a man who had a circle of students, meditating upon the significance of the Jewish religious tradition. Some fifty years later, the original author's grandson translated the book into Greek. It was written at a time when the Hebrew Bible as we know it today was coming into being, and the Jews who compiled the Biblical books were reflecting on the accumulations of story, imagery and wisdom which had found their way into their holy books.

The chapter draws upon the touching story in Genesis about the wooing of Rebekah. In Sirach, Wisdom is an emanation of God who looks round for somewhere to dwell, and finds that place in the tents of Jacob, in the Jewish inheritance. In Genesis, we find versions of the same story being written by at least two of the authors of these traditions. Old Abraham is about to die and wants a wife to be found for his son Isaac. He does not want Isaac to marry 'out', as Jews would later put it. Rather than finding a wife for him among the people of Canaan, where Abraham has settled, he asks a trusted servant to go back to his own country, to Aram-naharaim, to the city of Nahor. Laden with treasure and camels, the servant is commanded to offer to the chosen woman the chance to return to Canaan to marry Isaac. (In one version of the story, she is Abraham's niece, so Isaac would be marrying a cousin.) So the servant sets out, and when he reaches the city of Nahor, he makes the camels kneel down beside the well, as the women of the city are coming out to fetch water. Then he prays, 'Let the girl to whom I shall say, "Please offer your jar that I may drink," and who shall say, "Drink, and I will water your camels" – let her be the one whom you have appointed for your servant Isaac. By this I shall know that you have shown steadfast love to my master.' [Genesis 24:14] Steadfast love, Hebrew *hesed*, signifies the loyalty growing out of a friendship. God is asked to remember his side of a covenant with Abraham and with his people.

Before he has finished speaking, 'there was Rebekah, who was born to Bethuel son of Milcah, the wife of Nahor, Abraham's brother, coming out with her water jar on her shoulder. The girl was very fair to look upon, a virgin, whom no man had known.' [Genesis 24:15–16]

This beautiful, and virginal, woman was probably, for at least one of the authors of Genesis, J, already seen as a symbol of the Heavenly Wisdom visiting God's People. She was destined to become the mother of Israel, or, to give him his other name, of Jacob. In one of the versions in Genesis, written by E, the servant of Abraham goes to search for her, in the company of an angel.

The two stories – in Sirach and Genesis – are linked. Wisdom looks about for a place to dwell and finds it in Israel. Abraham, the father of the people of faith, looks about for a woman who will be willing to undertake the momentous task of becoming the mother of Israel, the Mother of the Faithful. She is, on the one hand, a simple virgin girl; on the other hand, she is Wisdom.

When two of the Gospel writers came to describe the coming of Jesus into the world, they drew on these two older stories, which had perhaps been written down two hundred years or so earlier, one a folk-tale shimmering with meaning, the other a Platonic myth about the arrival in the world of Wisdom itself. Luke speaks of the angel going to the virgin, Mary, and – as in the case of Rebekah – asking her to consent. This is so unlike the many stories in pagan antiquity of a young woman being raped by Zeus, either in his own person or in that of an animal. In this myth – and by using the word myth I do not mean to imply that it is untrue, but that it is a story carrying meaning – Mary is promised that if she consents, she will give birth to one who will be called the most high, 'He will reign over the house of Jacob forever' [Luke 1:33].

In the Fourth Gospel, the Prologue alludes to the tradition in Sirach of the Divine Logos, the Wisdom of God seeking lodgings among the human race, and coming among us.

In all three stories – Genesis, Sirach and Gospels – a gentle and feminine principle is introduced. The Wisdom, or the Word, is not simply something which comes to birth as a result of arid study, or of human effort. Likewise, those who respond to Christ are born, 'not of blood or of the will of the flesh or of the will of man, but of God' [John 1:13]. 'And she gave birth to her firstborn son and wrapped him in bands of cloth, and laid him in a manger, because there was no place for them in the inn.' [Luke 2:7]

It is appropriate that the mosaic in Hagia Sophia shows us the two emperors paying homage to the Virgin Mary. Constantine was the emperor who made the empire Christian. He convened the Council of Nicaea in 325, and it is from this Council that the Creed derives, subsequently recited in Christian liturgies, asserting that Christ was 'consubstantial' with the Father.

Justinian, two hundred years later, was a no less ardent champion of Orthodoxy, and a defender of the great Church Councils – Nicaea and Chalcedon. It was at Chalcedon that the Humanity of Christ was once again reasserted, against the many strange-minded groups who preached that the Divine Logos or Word had been no more than a Spirit, pretending to inhabit human form. No, said these Councils, he was a man, but a man who was of one being with the Father. This meant that the woman who bore him was the God-bearer, the Theotokos.

If the Gospels were what destructive fundamentalists might wish to make of them, historical writing of the post-Enlightenment era – that is, writings which could be 'verified', proved true or false – we should be astonished that so much honour is given by Christians to the Virgin Mary. After all, we 'know' so little about her. Are there not other women in history who are equally admirable? Only a few words, written in Greek on old papyrus, describe this Jewish girl. Compare that with the thousands of words we have to describe the achievements of, let us say, the Empress Catherine the Great, or the scientist Marie Curie, or Eleanor Roosevelt! About Mary we know almost nothing. The idea of Jesus being worshipped could inspire the same reaction. The implication is that Mary was called, by later generations, 'Mother of God', as a reward for being more 'impressive' than any of the other women of classical antiquity; or that Jesus was such an admirable man that it was not good enough to call him a saint or a great prophet.

This is not, historically, how the praise and worship of Jesus and his Mother are found to evolve. On the contrary, the 'simple prophet' of Galilee does not really make an appearance in the pages of history until the late eighteenth century in the writings of Rousseau and Thomas Jefferson. The New Testament writings *start* with the Hebrew stories of Wisdom, or the Word looking for a dwelling-place among men, among Israel. Similarly, Mary is honoured and revered throughout the Christian world, because the Word was made flesh at a particular moment in history, and as the result of a particular assent by a particular woman.

We will never know why the writers of the New Testament books thought it was appropriate to believe these things about Christ and his Mother, or to believe that the idea of the in-dwelling Wisdom of God, foreshadowed in the Genesis story of Rebekah or in the myth of Wisdom coming to dwell in Jacob's tent in Sirach, should have been chosen as the best way of describing the birth of Jesus.

The most extreme modern 'explanation' is to be found in the writings of those scholars who think that Jesus and Mary are simply literary constructs; that they never really existed *at all*. That they are, as it were, a pious piece of scissors and paste.

This idea, boldly outlined by a minority of New Testament scholars, has the attraction of simplicity. Since we cannot get behind the text, let us be content with – simply – the text. In a sense not intended by the Fourth Gospel, in the beginning was the Word – and the Word is all we have. (There is a much fuller discussion of this in the seventh chapter of this book, when we come to read the New Testament.)

Istanbul was a good place to be reading Gibbon. His mockery of the controversialists who squabbled about Christian doctrine, from Nicaea to Chalcedon and beyond, invites the civilized reader, from the comfortable position of modern rationalism, to collude in his contempt for their mental processes. 'The *Logos* is no longer a person, but an attribute; and it is only in a figurative sense, that the epithet of Son can be applied to the eternal reason which was with God from the beginning... Thus, after revolving round the theological circle, we are surprised to find... that the incomprehensible mystery which excites our adoration, eludes our inquiry.'

The Church of the Holy Wisdom was built to enshrine a liturgy which repeated the testimony. It was built five hundred years after Jesus was born, but it was not built in a vacuum. Between Jesus and the building of the church were five hundred years of human tradition. Some of those who handed on the tradition did so by writing. Others did so by dying, and their names were recorded as martyrs. Some, such as the Emperor Constantine, did so by asserting that the city itself, the polis, the world of human civic and political life, was consecrated to the Wisdom. After his conversion to Christianity, this Roman emperor summoned a Council at Nicaea in 325.

By then, it was nearly three hundred years since the time of the earthly Jesus, and what had begun as a small Jewish heresy, fiercely resisted by the mainstream of Judaism, and as a manifestation of Gentile monotheism half in touch, half uncomprehending of its Jewish roots, had grown to a movement which had spread all over the Mediterranean.

Constantine's conversion made possible the very existence of the Christian Bible. The Hebrew Scriptures had been collected in more or less the form, and order, which we know today by the second century BC – which is also when the Hebrew Scriptures were translated into Greek – known as the Septuagint because of the legend that seventy-two elders in Alexandria had translated the entire Hebrew Bible into Greek in seventy-two days. But the existence of a Christian 'canon' was not really finished until the second century AD, and most Christians studying the Scriptures would only have known a few books. There was not in existence a book with all the Old Testament and all of what we now call the New Testament in one codex. It was St Jerome (342–420) who changed that. He had studied at Rome and from 382 to 384 he was the secretary to Pope Damasus. But he then took off for the Levant, where he learnt Hebrew and lived an ascetic life as a quasi-hermit in the Syrian desert. Eventually, he felt his linguistic skill to be great enough to start work translating the Bible into Latin – the version known to posterity as the Vulgate. This book, which brought together the

Hebrew books of the old Jewish Scriptures with the Greek writings of the New Testament, was, as far as the West is concerned, the first Bible. That sense, which so possessed Northrop Frye, of the whole Bible being a single book, with a beginning and an ending, is made possible by Jerome's endeavour.

I liked the idea of L.'s Book of the People – a perspective of the Bible, not from the angle of the 'archaeologists' as she called them, but from those who had used the book, and whose lives had been touched by it. There were more ways of reading than just reading. The Emperor Justinian's church-building was a good example of this – the Monastery of St Catherine in Sinai, the wonders of the San Vitale mosaics in Ravenna, where Justinian and Theodora are represented surrounded not only by their councillors and lawmakers, but by the saints. When Dante lived in Ravenna and saw these wonders every day, they suggested to him the appearance of Justinian in the *Paradiso*.

> *Cesare fui e son Iustiniano,*
> *che, per voler del primo amor ch'i sento,*
> *d'entro le leggi trassi il troppo e' l vano*

> I was Caesar, and am Justinian,
> who, by the will of primal love, which I experience here in
>   Heaven,
> I purged our laws of emptiness and dross.

Justinian's achievements were immense – as a patron of great architecture, as a military conqueror. Gibbon and Dante would be united in acknowledgement of Justinian's genius as a lawgiver. It was he who, in fifty books, digested the miscellaneous laws of the territories and institutions over which he presided, and laid the foundation of 'Roman law' throughout Europe.

> The vain titles of the victories of Justinian are crumbled into dust; but the name of the legislator is inscribed on a fair and everlasting monument. Under his reign, and by his care, the civil jurisprudence was digested in the immortal works of the *Code*, the *Pandects* and the *Institutes*; the public reason of the Romans has been silently or studiously transfused into the domestic institutions of Europe, and the laws of Justinian still command the respect or obedience of independent nations.

After a day of swimming, it was delightful to repair, not to the great Hagia Sophia, with its armies of tourists, but to the place which has the nickname of the Little Hagia Sophia – the former church of Sts Sergius and Bacchus. Now it is a mosque, with a pleasant garden, set out with tea-tables and shaded by trees. In the cloister, there are even second-hand books for sale, though most of them are in Turkish.

The church was consecrated by the Emperor Justinian and the Ecumenical Patriarch on 27 December 537. Like the great Hagia Sophia, it has (hence its nickname) a tri-level domed core and two-storey niches whose walls open in column screens. On the columns, one sees the monograms of the Emperor Justinian and his wife Theodora, surely among the most unusual success stories in the political history of the world.

He was a Bulgarian peasant, whose soldier-uncle Justin became the Emperor. Justinian, who always spoke Greek with a 'barbarian' accent, emigrated from Dardania to Byzantium in his youth, and, after ingratiating himself with the court, the army and the Church, he was a good candidate to succeed his uncle. Perhaps the most remarkable fact about him, apart from his multifarious genius, was his choice of bride. He married Theodora, a prostitute and panto-mime-performer – the daughter of a bear-feeder in the hippodrome at Constantinople. 'The satirical historian has not blushed to describe the named scenes which Theodora was not ashamed to exhibit in the theatre. After exhausting the arts of sensual pleasure, she most ungratefully murmured against the parsimony of Nature; but her murmurs, her pleasures and her arts, must be veiled in the obscurity of a learned language.'

Yet this unlikely pair were united not only in love but in the desire to promote good and sound laws, imperial peace and Christian Orthodoxy. Theodora became very devout, and founded an insti-tution for the reform of the members of her former profession. (Some of the women were so unhappy that they threw themselves out of the windows into the sea.)

From the mosaic portrait in Ravenna, we can still sense her strength of character, and her allure. The pair reigned together until her death in 547. 'From his elevation to his death, Justinian governed the Roman empire thirty-eight years, seven months and thirteen days.'

There is a most extraordinary atmosphere of peace and prayer about this place.

Large numbers come each day for the evening prayers. My mind full of Gibbon's satirical debunking of Christian theology, there seemed to be a great dignity about these Muslim worshippers. 'Two things fill the mind with ever-increasing wonder and awe, the more often and the more intensely the mind of thought is drawn to them: the starry heavens above me and the moral law within me.' Isn't this enough? These Godfearing men and women who came each day to the mosque bowed down before the Ineffable mystery, but they had not burdened themselves with mythology. They were content to allow the Divine Wisdom to, as it were, float, without all the mess and inconvenience of making the Word take Flesh. There was great calm in the air as they prayed, and as we sipped our mint tea.

I remembered the passage of Gibbon which I had read that afternoon in which the warring factions of theological dispute divided between those who thought that Father and Son were Consubstantial – or of One Substance – *homoousios* – and those who believed that the Son was merely like the Father – *homoiousios*. 'The Greek word, which was chosen to express this mysterious resemblance, bears so close an affinity to the orthodox symbol, that the profane of every age have derided the furious contests which the difference of a single diphthong excited between the Homoousians and the Homoiousians.' I must have quoted this in a letter to L., perhaps comparing the two factions to the Big-Enders and Little-Enders in Swift's Lilliput, who dispute about how to eat boiled eggs. And was not the extraordinary thing about so many of these Christian controversies the fact that they so often reach the most furious heat when the matter under discussion is something which could never be demonstrated or proved?

But L. had written – most of the letter is lost, but I have one page of it as a bookmark in my Gibbon –

the Orthodox sound batty when lampooned; and no doubt they were, and can remain, very intolerant. But what would have happened to Christianity if one of the alternative versions had been triumphant? That Christ was a disembodied angel? A cult based on this view would rightly have fizzled out. The mind cannot absorb the Orthodox position – but what sort of pygmy-god do you want? One who can be absorbed and understood by a human mind? Surely the Councils, convoluted as their deliberations seem, and strange as their conclusions were, were trying to be true to the earlier testimony – to the New Testament beliefs, asserted over and over again, that though he was in the form of God, Christ was a man, who suffered under Pontius Pilate?

R., meanwhile, was reading a favourite novel, *The Towers of Trebizond* by Rose Macaulay, with its appropriately Turkish setting.

And this failure of the Christian Church, of every branch of it in every country, is one of the saddest things that has happened in all the world. But it is what happens when a magnificent idea has to be worked out by human beings who do not understand much of it but interpret it in their own way and think they are guided by God whom they have not yet grasped. And yet they had grasped something, so that the Church has always had great magnificence and much courage, and people have died for it in agony, which is supposed to balance all the other people who have had to die in agony because they did not accept it, and it has flowered up in learning and culture and beauty and art, to set against its darkness and incivility and obscurantism and barbarity and nonsense, and it has produced saints and martyrs and kindness and goodness, though these have also occurred freely outside it, and it is a wonderful and most extraordinary pageant of contradictions, and I, at least, want to be inside it, though it is foolishness to most of my friends.

JOB

We may take the Book of Job, perhaps, as the epitome of the narrative
of the Bible, as the Book of Revelation is the epitome of its imagery.

Northrop Frye, *The Great Code*

I CAME ACROSS L. during my first year at university. She was quite
a bit older than I was – a graduate student, working, as I came to
understand, on 'The Bible'. She happened to be sitting next to me in
a crowded lecture theatre in the newly built English Faculty Building
in Manor Road. The lecturer was the celebrated Canadian Northrop
Frye, who was spending a summer term in Oxford (where he had
himself studied as a graduate, at Merton College). He was lecturing
on William Blake. I had not then read Frye's ground-breaking
book on Blake, *Fearful Symmetry*, nor his *Anatomy of Criticism*. I
was therefore unprepared for his style: the huge magisterial sweep,
taking in the whole of world history; the vast Vico-esque, not to say
Spenglerian, generalizations, and divisions of the ages of man, the

preoccupations with myth and language. I came in time to see what an enormous influence Frye had had on L., and in turn – both via L. and in my own reading of him – what a great influence he would have on the way I myself read the world. At the time of these Blake lectures, Frye had not yet published his superb book on the Bible, *The Great Code*, which took its title from Blake's 'The Old and New Testaments are the Great Code of Art'.

Frye seemed to have absorbed much of Blake's prophetic mantle, not a little of his sheer battiness. His lectures on Blake were a stylish pyrotechnic display. He began each of them with a resumé of what he had said in the previous week, but instead of saying, 'Last time, we were discussing. . .', he would declaim: 'Last Day. . .' and there would then be a longish pause. During the ten seconds before more words came forth, there was time to wonder whether he was himself a recording angel, dispatched to Oxford to announce the End of Time itself, and the ushering in of the Rule of the Saints.

Quite by chance, L. was sitting beside me at the first lecture, much of which had passed over my head, as Frye discoursed of Blake's Prophetic Books (which I found impenetrable), illustrated with diagrams which he chalked rapidly on the board, talking all the time and letting forth a truly prodigious range of reference. Everything from Milton to Hegel, from Luther to Kant, from Giambattista Vico to the Tibetan Book of the Dead, was apparently of relevance.

In those days, L. had dark hair. She looked like a sad gypsy. At – what, seven? – years older than I was, her intense, innocent, bony face was much as it remained for the next thirty-plus years of our friendship. The same aquiline nose, the same high cheekbones, the same intense dark eyes which glinted behind very thick specs.

Typically of L., she turned to me after the lecture, without introducing herself, and started in with that conversation which we continued until she died, sometimes in person, sometimes by letter or postcard, and sometimes by a weird telepathy, which would mean that she would simply materialize in my life – often after an absence, and a silence, of several years – and meet my mind at the point which it had reached in my own puzzled searching of the Scriptures.

—It's bold, his – Frye's – view that the Bible was to be read as a whole. Biblical 'scholarship' as such is of very limited use in appreciating the Bible. Frye always says that the very worst way to read the Bible is as an anthology of Near Eastern texts, some written before, some after Christ.

—But isn't that precisely what the Bible *is*? I don't know how you can read a book 'as a whole' which has so many different authors, was composed at so many different times. . . Take Genesis alone. No scholar knows whether the Yahwist author is the oldest strand – as used to be thought. Then there is the Priestly author, and the Eloist author. . . and all their different narratives coalesce and have been shoved together by a redactor to form the book we know as Genesis.

—That's all very well, said L. —But that sort of work is really archaeology, not reading. Isn't the fascination of the Bible the story of how it has been read, how it has been interpreted? The way it has shaped human lives, human imaginations? The Bible is a great work of the imagination.

—But whose imagination, the reader's or the writers'?

—That is the question! Some coffee?

When she stood, I saw how very tall she was, a good six feet two.

I did not know at the time, though I discovered in the course of that term – when Frye gave those eight unforgettable lectures on Blake – that L. had actually begun her graduate work at Toronto, as a pupil of Frye's, and this was the origin of her elusive 'Bible book'. She spoke of it to me during that summer in Oxford as if it was a work all but completed.

—Take Job, she said to me a few weeks later as we were walking around Christ Church Meadows. —Tell me what you know about it.

—Well, I said, it's one of the great literary masterpieces of the Bible. Probably written at the time of the Exile – 600 or so, maybe 500 BC.

—That's the archaeology out of the way, said L. —But, you must see, in effect Job is the whole of the Bible in miniature. Job foreshadows it all. Remember, Job was 'the greatest of all the men of the east'. He's a type of virtuous, perfect man – almost a king. In the first chapter the wholly virtuous Job loses his ten children – seven sons and three daughters – his extensive flocks of sheep, his camels and all his wealth. In the second chapter, he finds himself covered in sores. We, the readers, or hearers of the tale, are aware that these calamities have befallen a blameless, religious man as the result of an almost frivolous debate between God, Yahweh and Satan, who in the Hebrew is described as one of the sons of God. Yahweh believes that, whatever is thrown at him, Job will not lose his faith. Satan is of the opinion that if Job is made to suffer enough, he will abandon his faith. 'Does Job fear God for nothing?' [Job 1:9]

Satan's question is one of the big questions of the book. And it is, of course, a great book, one of the Biblical books which is also a stupendous work of literature, a book in which the Hebrew poetry is never more hauntingly musical or sad, nor in which the theological questions, now simple to the point of simple-mindedness, now subversive and deep, are more disturbing.

Christians who believe that the Bible contains all the answers to all the questions are as likely to be disturbed by the Book of Job as those anti-Godders who want to think that the Bible is a sort of Koran, designed to hammer you over the head with instructions about how to live. By contrast, the really disturbing thing about the Book of Job, as about the Bible as a whole, is its refusal to answer the questions which it so honestly and devastatingly puts.

You will remember that in the Book of Genesis, Abraham and the Lord have a conversation about the sinful city of Sodom. God is in favour of total destruction, but he has to warn Abraham to get out first, since it is in Abraham's seed that all the future generations of the blessed will be found. But, asks Abraham, supposing there were fifty righteous people left in Sodom? How about that? Would you destroy a whole city and risk killing fifty righteous? And so on, until he has whittled down the number from forty-five to twenty to ten. In this conversation, who is the righteous one? Abraham, with his sense of justice, or the impetuous God who seemingly rains down destruction upon the just and the unjust?

We think of this exchange throughout the Book of Job, especially at the end, when having seen off his irritating and unhelpful friends Eliphaz, Bildad and Zophar, and the pious young Elihu, Job is confronted by God himself. Throughout the book, the friends have been trying to persuade Job that the reason for his misfortunes is that he must, somehow or other, have committed some wrongdoing, for which God is justly punishing him. And Job is equally insistent that he has *not* deserved his punishment, not done anything wrong, and indeed lived righteously. Then comes God's great poem at the end, from Chapter 38 onwards, 'Where wast thou when I laid the foundations of the earth?'

Job does not know, as we the hearers or readers know, that the reason for his sufferings are in a sense frivolous – not quite to settle a bet, but to settle a dispute between God and one of his sons. He hears God out. God represents himself as the Lord of the natural universe, of the seas, of the sinewy horse and the locust, of the soaring hawk and the mighty whale, the great Leviathan. Job submits to God. 'Therefore have I uttered that I understood not; things too wonderful for me, which I knew not.' [Job 42:3] He abases himself in dust and ashes. God then rewards him by allowing him to have ten more children, the firstborn of whom is named Jemimah, as well as a great number of sheep, camels, oxen and donkeys and one hundred and forty more years of life. . .

I have made this into a discourse. Probably L. said such things to me on several walks, and during several conversations over cups of coffee after Frye had given his Blake lectures.

I remember one other thing she 'hammered home' during that phase of our friendship.

—The three irritating friends, and the wife of Job all think that *he* is on trial. But it is a much more revolutionary book than that. Job makes it quite clear – he has done nothing wrong. All he asks is to be released from his torments by a merciful death. But even as he indulges in his (in a way) pointless debates with the pious friends, it is clear that Job is not on trial. Someone else is, though. God thinks that he has settled the matter by his great poem at the end – 'Where wast thou when I laid the foundations of the earth?' [Job 38:4] But he has not settled anything. Job, in many a lyrical passage, has acknowledged that God is responsible for the world order as we know it. The great poem in Job 28, about the elusiveness of Wisdom, seems when you first read it as if he is asking how can a human being become wise? 'Whence then cometh wisdom? And where is the place of understanding? Seeing it is hid from the eyes of all living, and kept close from the fowls of the air?' [Job 28:20–21]

But does the personification, the mythologization of Wisdom make him or her personal? Isn't Job saying, we know about the big, powerful Creator-God who made whales and earthquakes, who rains down abundance and calamity on the earth in equal and indifferent supply. But we can't learn anything from such a God – he's really just a name for the forces of Nature, and his punishment of completely virtuous people makes him a figure who is unknowable – and if he were knowable, would we be as virtuous as Job and worship him? 'Behold, God is great, and we know him not.' [Job 36:26]

Job has laid some other time-bombs for us too. About death, he has been uncompromising. It is the end. There is nothing beyond it. Death is 'a land of darkness, as darkness itself; and of the shadow of death, without any order, and where the light is as darkness' [Job 10:22].

But then, in Chapter 19, he starts off on another tack. 'Oh that my words were now written! Oh that they were printed in a book! That they were graven with an iron pen and lead in the rock for ever! For I know that my redeemer liveth, and that he shall stand at the latter day upon the earth: And though after my skin worms destroy this body, yet in my flesh shall I see God' [Job 19:23–26]. Maestro!

Cue for Handel's *Messiah*. What a good example of how the Bible is the only book which does not merely gain from translation, it is in some ways the *creation* of translators. Not only have the 1611 translators created the wonderful anachronism of Job, two thousand years before Gutenberg's invention, wishing that his words could be printed in a book. With equal disregard for the contemporary meaning of the word, they make Job into a Christian who knows that his redeemer liveth. The Hebrew *go'el* was translated by the Authorized Version translators as 'redeemer'. When the word is used in Numbers 35:19 and Deuteronomy 19:6 it means an avenger of blood, the nearest male family member who would vindicate his relative's wrongs. The *go'el* also redeemed lost or misappropriated family property. The phrase is charged with near-blasphemous irony, since etymologically *go'el* seems to mean something like 'a bit like God'. Job, however, is calling for an Avenger to call God to account for his misdeeds. He also seems (though this is more dubious) to be implying that the only way in which he could find any consolation for his appalling sufferings was if he could be given a chance after death to see Justice. But the things he has said previously suggest that he does not believe in life after death. So the 'Avenger' who lives, to call God to account. . . who is he? Is he a product of Job's fantasy? A creature of wish-fulfilment? Or has the human race moved on while this great genius of a poet has been at work and started to believe in Life after Death?

⌘

Shortly after that conversation with L. about Job, the term came to an end. L. left Oxford, and I did not see her for several years.

I did not have an address to write to. She wrote a postcard to my college. It contained no expression of pleasure that we had begun a friendship, if that was what we had done, nor of regret that we were now to be separated, as she went on to whatever the next stage was for her. (In fact, a spell as a supply teacher in a rough school in Reading, followed by what seems to have been some sort of mental collapse or nervous breakdown.) Her card, closely written, simply read:

Israel. The etymology. The Hebrew *sarah* means to fight or to wrestle. The story of Jacob wrestling with the angel in Genesis 32:24–30. Jacob and his two wives, his menservants and his eleven sons were journeying. Jacob found himself alone with a stranger with whom he wrestled. As dawn broke, the man asked to be released. Jacob said he would not release him until he blessed him.

'So he said to him, "What is your name?" And he said, "Jacob." Then the man said, "You shall no longer be called Jacob, but Israel, for you have striven with God and with humans and have prevailed."' [Genesis 32:27–28]

Israel means 'The man who strives against God' – or perhaps 'God fights'. Wonderfully uncosy. This the subject not only of Job but of *entire Bible*.

It was probably twenty years after receiving that card that I found myself in Edinburgh at festival time, and drawn to the exhibition of Blake's drawings from the Book of Job at the National Gallery of Scotland. L. was clutching a little green book – one of the two volumes of the plays of Sophocles in the Loeb edition, translated by Hugh Lloyd-Jones. There was no 'Hello', or 'What a surprise seeing you, after two or three years'.

—Lloyd-Jones reminds us, L. said, that there are two approaches to the tragedies. There are those who see them as stories by which heroes must learn wisdom through suffering, since the divine government of the universe is necessarily just; and those who see Ajax and Philoctetes and Oedipus as great figures, virtuous figures who defy the cruel whims of unjust Gods.

Now the strange thing about the Book of Job is that it demands, I think – because of the prose preface – to be read as the second sort of book – that is, it demands to be seen as the exemplary and dignified behaviour of a man who has heroic patience in the face of appalling injustice unleashed upon him by Satan and by God. And yet, it attributes to God, not only in the foolish utterances of the Comforters, but in the great closing passages, virtues which are lacking in the Olympian immortals, a moral seriousness which we do not invariably find even in the elevated Sophoclean deities.

God by the end of this book seems to belong largely to the world of Nature. He has become almost Spinoza's *Deus sive Natura*, the process by which storms, locusts, whales etc. come to pass. He cannot ask Job's awestruck obedience before the force which creates whales and oceans, without seeing that this makes him the God of tsunamis, earthquakes and famines.

The Book of Job, L. concluded, says that our awe in the face of Nature does not alter the question of how we should be living decent lives. For most of our contemporaries, that decent or good life is lived today without religion. Not for them either the unanswerable question of how God could allow a tsunami or a child's death by leukaemia.

Earlier in a letter, L. had written to me:

Job is the central book of the Bible. It is not a book to finish and lay by, it is a book to wrestle with, to be troubled by. There will be days when the figures within it seem like spectres in a nightmare.

The narrator, the poet of the book, represents God not only as the source of wisdom and strength, but also as a capricious and in a way heartless figure. God almost needs Job, the virtuous, patient Job, to show what the Good Life is, or could be.

The Book of Job does not only stand at the centre of the Bible. It is in a way the whole of the Bible in miniature. For, having tried to wrestle, throughout the Old Testament, with the problem of Omnipotence and Love – the problem of how you could posit a loving Creator in the utter misery of the world, the Bible comes up with a radical solution. In Job we have God, the thunderingly clumsy upholder of natural order and justice; we have Job, the virtuous human being who simply suffers calamity after calamity; and we have the infusion of elusive Wisdom – where is Wisdom to be found? – which tries to make sense of the tragedy. In the second half of the Bible, the New Testament, these things coalesce in one figure, Jesus. Job is a type of Jesus and the Book of Job is a type of Gospel. Bonhoeffer said he could only worship a suffering God. Job anticipates, indeed helps to create, a religion which holds together the apparent incompatibilities – God the Author of things as they are – the Father; God the source of Wisdom, the Spirit. And in the tormented human archetype – this surely is the Bible's genius – in humanity at its most abject, most vulnerable, most unjustly tormented – especially here, it finds the divine. Thereby it seeks, even in the most terrible calamities of war, earthquake, disease and waste, to find divinity in each abandoned Japanese corpse, each fly-blown African child, each anonymous, childish owner of the shoes which piled up in the Nazi death camps, each skull heaped up by Pol Pot.

But now we were in Edinburgh, at an exhibition of Blake's engravings of the Book of Job.

I must have 'looked at' these pictures before somewhere, perhaps reproduced in books about Blake. But I had never really 'seen' them. I was in the position of Blake's Job himself, who, only towards the end of the sequence, begins to understand: 'I have heard thee with the hearing of the Ear but now my Eye seeth thee' (Illustration XVII), a print in which Job and his wife kneel to be blessed by God. They are not looking at him, however, they are staring into the middle distance. The friends, presumably his Comforters, are terrified, and sit with their back to God, cowering in darkness, with their faces covered. Only after he has learnt to 'see' can Job pray. The last four pictures show, in turn: Job with outstretched arms praying to the Light; Job and his wife having the humility to accept charity from others – dispossessed, he has learnt the meaning of Love; Job telling the story of his Life to his daughters, a scene not in the Biblical text – this is a key picture, because it illustrates Blake's belief that, as he wrote in *The Laocoön*, 'Art is the Tree of Life' and 'Christianity is Art'; and finally, Job, his wife and his new family restored to prosperity. They are not praying in the pious mode of conventional churchgoers, as they were in the very first illustration. They are making music beneath the cosmic tree. They have entered the realm of the imagination.

In his preface to *Jerusalem*, Blake had written, 'I know of no other Christianity and of no other Gospel than the liberty both of body and mind to exercise the Divine Arts of Imagination. . . O ye Religious, discountenance every one among you who shall pretend to despise Art and Science! I call upon you in the Name of Jesus! What is the life of Man but Art and Science?'

Blake's reading of Job is truly revolutionary. His Job, unlike L.'s or that of conventional Christianity, is that, in a sense, the Comforters are right. Job, in the first illustration, when he is piously conventional and conventionally pious, is not alive. He cannot see. The musical instruments hang unplayed in the tree above his head. In the frame beneath, Blake has drawn an altar on which are written the words from 2 Corinthians 3:6, 'The Letter Killeth. The Spirit giveth Life.' Job has not received the Spirit. To this extent, he could not be more wrong in his belief that he is without fault. He has a single vision. He cannot see into the life of things. 'May God us keep', Blake prayed with his friend Thomas Butts, 'From Single Vision & Newton's Sleep.'

The subsequent illustrations are among the most disturbing artworks I have ever seen. As in other Blake paintings and engravings, the figure of Satan, deriving from his own reading of

Milton's heroic depiction, is a classically beautiful figure, large, vibrant, muscular, a Farnese Hercules come to life. This is a winged demi-god who destroys the sons of Job and brings the pillars of their palace tumbling about them.

The depiction of Job's Evil Dreams is especially imaginative and troubling. Job lies flat, his eyes wide open, his face contorted with fear. God, whose hair has been shaped in a curious star-like crown, leans over him to illustrate the text 'With Dreams upon my bed thou scarest me & affrightest me with Visions'. But God himself is cloven-footed and entwined with a serpent. He is a Satanic God. What Blake appears to be saying is that Job can still not see that he has invented his God. His God is a sort of devil. He began as the defender of the proprieties and the conventions, but now he is a sort of cosmic monster who can only affright him. This God is not just the conventional God of 'Religion', the God for whom men and women put on their smartest clothes to worship on a Sunday morning as a way of feeling good about themselves, their sexual normality, their wealth, their comfort. He is also the bogus God of the Philosophers, the God of the Creationists and the Theorists, the God whose existence can be proved. And if he exists, then indeed he would be a devil, for he would be the God who created Evil. The true God, who speaks to Job out of the whirlwind, 'who maketh the Clouds his Chariot & walketh on the Wings of the Wind', is a strange, bearded, swirling figure (Illustration XIII) whose long beard, sad, attentive face, and long expressive hands are in fact all but identical to those of Job himself.

I do not remember when L. spoke to me the words I have attributed to her in an earlier part of this chapter. I know that she came round the exhibition with me, and I know that we went for coffee somewhere afterwards. I noticed her hands were shaking as she lifted the cup to her lips, mid-sentence, and – unable to get to the end of her thought – she replaced it in the saucer. This she did over and over again, as a light skin formed on the surface of the cup.

I was speechless, because the Blake exhibition was one of the few aesthetic experiences of my life which was palpably life-changing (another was the first time my wife R. and I attended *The Ring of the Nibelungs*). I could feel myself changing as I looked at those pictures, and I could not immediately take in what L. was saying, because I was so aware of what Blake was saying.

Northrop Frye's comment on the first and last of the illustrations sums up what was happening to me. 'In the last plate, things are much as they were before, but Job's family have taken the instruments down from the tree and are playing them. In Blake, we recover our original state, not by returning to it, but by re-creating it. The act of creation, in its turn, is not producing something out of nothing, but the act of setting free what we already possess.'

Blake, who read deeply in Kabbalistic literature, Swedenborg, the Gnostics and so on, was almost self-consciously a 'heretic'. Maybe he had to do that, rather than try to fit his ideas into any of the conventional churches or chapels of his day. What these pictures made so clear to me that day – it is so obvious that I feel sheepish at admitting to being so bowled over, so surprised! – is the absolute centrality of the imagination as a key to perception. The Job illustrations are a shout of protest against the 'scientific outlook' as well as a demolition of conventional religion. The former believed it had abolished the Bible, by treating the Bible as a series of improbable histories, lazy substitutes for scientific theories and outmoded religious, dietary and sexual 'laws'. The latter responded, disastrously, by entirely accepting the premises of the Enlightenment. Ignoring the text at the bottom of Blake's first picture of Job – 'The Letter Killeth . . .' – they began to treat the Bible as if it were all the things which it is not. They refused to see the living power of Myth.

This is not just a 'lit. crit.' perception. It is the way the Bible has actually 'worked' in human life. The example in Chapter Three, of Dr King and the Civil Rights Movement, is only one, extremely vivid case in point. Since the eighteenth century, among the slaves on the Southern plantations, there had developed the imaginative identification of their plight with that of the Hebrew slaves in Egypt. Building upon such tropes, and upon the whole Old Testament mythology of deliverance – of the Hebrews from Egypt, of the exiled Jews from Babylon – King had at his disposal a shared rhetoric, one to which millions of people, steeped in the Book, could respond. The words, when he quoted them, resonated because he was applying them in the way they had always been applied in times when the Spirit gave life. In earlier ages, and later, Christians had used the mythology of Deliverance as a picture of what happened to the individual soul, as when Dante, about to explore Purgatory, hears the delivered souls, as they come over the water piloted by the Angel, singing Psalm 114: 'When Israel went out of Egypt, the house of Jacob from a people of strange language'.

Those imprisoned in the 'Letter', in the literal reading of the Bible, would waste their time wondering whether the Children of Israel, as a matter of historical fact, ever set foot in Egypt, or whether they had ever crossed the desert, and if so, when, and in what numbers.

And literalists on one side would think they had defended the 'truth' of the Bible by saying that this stuff was 'history', while the other side mocked, or politely smiled. Meanwhile, on fire with the prophetic spirit, Martin Luther King had changed the world. The Spirit giveth Life.

Once again, we turn back to the very beginning of the Bible and wonder if the literalists have even begun to ask themselves what is meant by the verses 'Then God said, "Let us make humankind in our image, according to our likeness"' [Genesis 1:26], and again, 'the Lord God formed man from the dust of the ground, and breathed into his nostrils the breath of life; and the man became a living being' [Genesis 2:7], and again, after Adam and Eve have eaten the apple and learnt the knowledge of good and evil, 'the lord God said, "See, the man has become like one of us, knowing good and evil"' [Genesis 3:22].

Rather than allowing these words to infuse their imaginations, some human beings would prefer to read the Bible 'literally', deriving from it not just false impressions, but shutting themselves off, not merely from an understanding of the Bible, but an understanding of anything at all. Humanity, divinely made and divinely inspired, lives in the realm of the imagination. Language itself is metaphor. Materialism or Reductionism, or whatever you call it, the most boring, as well as the least accurate way of experiencing the world and recording experience, is the dominant mindset of the Western intelligentsia in our day. They think they have disposed of the 'evidence' of the Bible when they have 'proved' that there was no such person as Noah, or that Jonah, having spent three days in the belly of a fish, would probably have died of asphyxiation. Perhaps satisfyingly to themselves, they have created a century-long nervous breakdown among religious believers who think that in order to 'defend' their religion, they ought to keep silent about one of the most obvious facts about the Bible, namely that it is mythology. (Nor is this phenomenon restricted to the Bible belt, or the unsophisticated by-ways of American Protestantism. Which academic examiner was it who did not allow Thomas L. Thompson his doctorate because he dared to question the historicity of Abraham? Step forward Joseph Ratzinger!)

Before we parted in Edinburgh that day, L. said,

—Go steady on Blake. I can see he has 'got' to you. He was basically a Gnostic.

—Thanks for the warning.

The skin was still floating on her cold coffee as we paid the waitress. I watched her tall back wandering up Princes Street and disappear into the crowds. Her bob of hair was grey now. Strange that I had not noticed this as we talked – I suppose I had been so mesmerized by her dark eyes that I had not had time to notice her hair. It was, as it happened, the last time I ever saw her, though we exchanged cards and letters for a year or two more.

I have not taken L.'s advice about going steady on Blake. The more I read him, and the more I look at his paintings and engravings, the more it seems he anticipated, with quite prodigious accuracy and intuition, all the more bizarre delusions of our times. The deeper his messages sank into my soul, the more I wished to read the Bible with the eyes of the imagination, the more glorious it seemed; and also, the more dangerous it seemed, to read it in a materialistic or literal way. The revulsion I felt 'against religion' twenty years ago grew in intensity, the more I felt the enemies of religion, like poor old H. – now dead from throat cancer – to be barking up the wrong tree.

Indeed, the last time I heard H.'s voice was on the radio, indulging in one of those impassioned rants of his. He was saying that you did not have to go further down the alphabet than the letter B, in itemizing the world's trouble-spots, in order to see the harm done by religion. I forget the Bs now – they included Belfast, where Catholics and Protestants were (at the time I heard the broadcast) still knocking hell out of one another; Baghdad, where Sunnis and Shiites were fighting it out; and Bethlehem in the land of Judah, then divided by a Berlin-style concrete wall.

There would once have been a time when the emotional revulsion of H. against all the disgusting human behaviour on display in those towns would certainly have made me draw the false inference – what do they all have in common? Religion. How do we make the world a better place? Get rid of religion. Now, it seems pretty obvious that what they all have in common is that they are inhabited by human beings. That human beings have an ineluctable tendency to think materially, and literally, and that this is a sort of death. Were things any better before the Enlightenment, when men and women went to war, literally, over the question of how, or whether, Christ was present in the Eucharist? Of course not. But are we going to throw away all our religious inheritance, and two and a half thousand years of shared reading of the Bible, because we can't be bothered to read it imaginatively?

SIX

LIVING IN A
METAPHOR: PSALMS

Go search this thing,
Tumble thy breast, and turn thy book.

George Herbert, 'The Method'

STUCK IN MY Bible at the beginning of Psalms, I find a letter L. had written to me once:

Just seen a man outside the subway near Washington Square, wearing a sandwich board which reads: PRAYER IS TALKING TO YOURSELF!

'I call upon you, for you will answer me, O God' [Psalm 17:6] – though I prefer the Gelineau translation – 'I am here and I call, you will hear me, O God' [Psalm 16 in Gelineau]... This human capacity to talk to God. The belief that he listens – even, that he will reply! In the early stories, especially those written by J, this can be explained by simple anthropomorphism. Yahweh walks about, gets angry, changes his mind, and so forth. As the books of the Bible are at present arranged, God (or whichever of the Gods you are thinking of, Yahweh, Elohim, El Shaddai, and so on) talks quite freely to people in the patriarchal times. Less often in the times of the kings – hence the value of the prophets who, so to say, speak *for* Yahweh. Their mouths speak his words. The last time God actually 'appeared' to a human being, in the Bible stories, is when he had his conversation with Solomon [1 Kings 9:2].

When he appeared to the King, the Lord said:

'I have heard your prayer and your plea, which you made before me; I have consecrated this house that you have built, and put my name there forever; my eyes and my heart will be there for all time. . . If you turn aside from following me, you or your children. . . but go and serve other gods and worship them, then I will cut Israel off from the land that I have given them. . . and Israel will become a proverb and a taunt among all peoples.' [1 Kings 9:3,6,7]

Which of course is what happens – Solomon has no sooner built the Temple than he starts to worship other gods and the whole catastrophe begins. Thereafter Yahweh deserts the scene. Interesting book called *The Disappearance of God* by Richard Elliott Friedman, relating these Bible stories to later 'death of God' ideas – Nietzsche and so on. . . and all the American crazies like Altizer (Alzheimer??!) in the '60s.

When were the tales of Solomon written down? Probably about 600, 620 BC? By the Deuteronomic author? Or do we go for the much later date favoured by Thompson in *The Bible in History*? Either way, it's a sophisticated idea that a whole people can lose touch with their God, he can just withdraw. Rather like the death of a relationship, end of a marriage when one partner starts seeing another person?

But while all this is going on in Bible literature, we also have the growth of personal religion in the Psalms? It's a bit like what we talked of in Philadelphia, when you were discovering Wallace Stevens/ the death of images, the washing of language. Atheism a clearer path to the true God than conventional religion, because it is clearing the mind of cant, as Dr Johnson said. Our old friend Simone again – *Entre deux hommes qui n'ont pas l'expérience de Dieu, celui qui le nie en est peut-être le plus près*...

It more than once struck me over the years that L. was modelling herself on Simone Weil – the intensity, the bookishness, the uncompromisingness, the self-conscious poverty. Whereas Simone Weil's life was perforce adrift – because of the Second World War – L.'s wanderings were, so far as I could tell, self-imposed. She could have accepted a full-time teaching post somewhere, rather than always doing supply work, and moving on after a few months. The extent of the mental illness? The periodic 'breakdowns' were perhaps her real reason for never holding down a job. And she had once shocked me when unable to recall a name, blaming her memory loss on 'that damned ECT they made me have once upon a time'.

About ten years ago, I received a letter from the Reverend Mother of a small Roman Catholic religious community near Salisbury in Wiltshire.

> We have been unable to find any trace of a family, but some letters from yourself were found tucked into her Bible. She appears to have had very few possessions – her luggage in the Guest House here contained only a change of clothes, the Bible, and a copy of George Herbert's poems. She was found dead at the back of the chapel after Compline on Tuesday evening last week. The cause of death appears to have been a heart attack. The doctor who looks after this community managed to trace her medical records through the wonders of the computer. She was fifty-five – as I am sure you knew. Naturally, it has been a great shock to us all. Though none of us ever got to know her well, we had grown fond of her and looked forward to her visits. We understand that she was an Anglican, so the funeral was conducted by the Rector of Bemerton – George Herbert's parish, as you may know. We thought this would be appropriate. Two of the sisters and myself were glad to be able to attend the funeral. No one else was there. I am sorry we were unable to locate an address for you in time to tell you of the ceremony. It was a very simple service. I went with the Rector to the Crematorium afterwards...

I read through that letter from L. again, with its somewhat gnomic quotation from the notebooks of Simone Weil. 'Of the two men with no experience of God, it is perhaps the man who denies him who is the closer to him.'

The trouble with this 'shocking' idea of Weil's is that it begs the question of what an experience of God might be. How would you know that you had had an experience of God, rather than simply imagining that you had done so?

Weil's own conversion, after all, took place not in a literary vacuum, but while she was reciting a poem – George Herbert's 'Love'. In her excellent biography, Weil's friend Simone Pétrement recalled, 'Here we are astonished ourselves and are brought, as it were, to a standstill by the account of an event that remains impenetrable to us. It surprises us as much as the event surprised her. It is hard to understand why, given her ideas until that moment, she did not regard this feeling of Christ's presence as a purely subjective impression; why she thought Christ had really been present.'

> Love bade me welcome: yet my soul drew back,
>   Guiltie of dust and sinne.
> But quick-ey'd Love, observing me grow slack
>   From my first entrance in,
> Drew nearer to me, sweetly questioning,
>   If I lack'd any thing.
>
> 'A guest,' I answer'd, 'worthy to be here:'
>   Love said, 'You shall be he.'
> 'I, the unkinde, ungratefull? Ah, my deare,
>   I cannot look on thee.'
> Love took my hand, and smiling did reply,

'Who made the eyes but I?'

'Truth, Lord; but I have marr'd them: let my shame
    Go where it doth deserve.'
'And know you not,' says Love, 'who bore the blame?'
    'My deare, then I will serve.'
'You must sit down,' says Love, 'and taste my meate.'
    So I did sit and eat.

Weil's conversion, her sense that Christ was palpably present to her when she read this poem, is itself a real literary parcel or palimpsest. For she felt herself confronted by the true God when reading a poem. The poetry of Herbert itself, at one and the same time highly original and completely artful, is a reading of that book of the Bible which more than any other dramatizes the inner life, gives expression to our own direct experiences of God: Psalms. Herbert is one of the noblest and cleverest examples of a great imagination, and a developed poetic master, reading the Bible.

Were it ever to fall to me to write L.'s book for her, Herbert would certainly be one of my 'People' of whom the Bible is the Book. Not only did his poetry grow from the mulch of the Bible, but his life was shaped by daily recitations of the Bible.

Born in 1593, of distinguished Welsh gentry, Herbert was part of a large family. His father died when he was three years old. His mother, born Magdalen Newport, had no fewer than ten children – seven sons and three daughters, '*Iobs* number and *Iobs* distributions as she her selfe would often remember'. The words are those of John Donne who lodged in her house after she had remarried – to Sir John Danvers. Intelligent, witty, intensely pious, Magdalen was an exemplary mother, who was largely responsible for the education of her children until they were eligible for school. George Herbert attended Westminster School, where he came under the influence of the Dean of Westminster, Lancelot Andrewes, and Trinity College, Cambridge. At the university, his intelligence was matched by his ambition. He became the Public Orator and had ambitions to succeed not only in the academic but in the political world. He aspired to a high position at court.

Following the death of James I, however, and a series of illnesses, Herbert changed direction. He took Holy Orders when in his early thirties and, having married Jane Danvers, a relation of his stepfather's, he settled in the village of Bemerton, near Salisbury, and near Wilton, the seat of his cousin, the Earl of Pembroke. The aloof, haughty Public Orator of Cambridge became a model pastor. Accessible to all his humble parishioners, he became their friend. He patched up quarrels between them. He urged them to read. He administered simple physic to them. Twice a day, he read the Office in his little church, nearly always attended by a congregation. *The Book of Common Prayer* lays down that the priest should read through more or less the whole Bible in the course of a year, and the Psalms every month. These portions of Scriptures are divided up, and supplemented with prayers, to form what Anglicans call Matins and Evensong – a truncated version of the old Monastic Hours of Prayer from the Roman Breviary. 'Holy Mr Herbert', as he came to be known locally, became a type of the English parish priest whose example has inspired thousands since.

He died in March 1633 when he was not yet forty. He will always be remembered for his sanctity of life. He also left behind the volume of verse contained in the book known as *The Temple*. Rhetorically sharp, dramatic and personal, the poems lay naked and raw an intense life of prayer. It is easy to see how Weil could have felt the presence of Christ as she read Herbert's 'Love' since this is what the poem itself does: it conveys so very powerfully what it felt like to be praying to Christ and receiving his consoling presence.

Herbert's poems are palimpsests, in which it is difficult – impossible, in fact, for they are so carefully wrought – to distinguish between their rhetoric and the realities they describe. The prophets spoke with the Divine Afflatus, and it was under this inspiration that Christian prophets since have spoken – such figures as Dr Martin Luther King not so much quoting the Old Testament prophets (though he did so) as embodying the Old Testament, enfleshing it, making it happen in our midst.

This way of reading the Bible as typology was second nature to Herbert, never more overt than in his poem 'The Bunch of Grapes'. The title refers to the moment in the Book of Numbers (Chapters 13–14) when scouts, who have been sent to spy out the land of Canaan, return to the Israelites in the wilderness, bearing a bunch of grapes on a single pole carried between them. The poem begins with the speaker's own mood swings, his own mental state, which is immediately read in terms of the journeying of the Israelites in the wilderness.

> Joy, I did lock thee up: but some bad man
>   Hath let thee out again:
> And now, me thinks, I am where I began
>   Sev'n years ago: one vogue and vein,
>   One aire of thoughts usurps my brain.
> I did towards Canaan draw; but now I am
> Brought back to the Red sea, the sea of shame.

For as the Jews of old by Gods command
    Travell'd, and saw no town:
So now each Christian hath his journeys spann'd:
    Their storie pennes and sets us down.
    A single deed is small renown.
God's works are wide, and let in future times;
His ancient justice overflowes our crimes.

Then have we too our guardian fires and clouds;
    Our Scripture-dew drops fast:
We have our sands and serpents, tents and shrowds;
    Alas! our murmurings come not last.
    But where's the cluster? Where's the taste
Of mine inheritance?

The experience of reading the Bible becomes a way of reading off our own experiences and backslidings and emotional life against the template of the Myth. And you can see it working. Not merely 'working' rhetorically in the terms of Herbert's poetics, but in terms of human lives. 'The poet invents the metaphor, and the Christian lives it', as R. S. Thomas brilliantly put it in the preface to his own selection of Herbert's poems.

In no other book of Scripture is this more the case than in Psalms. This hymnbook of the synagogue, this anthology of some of the most sublime religious poetry in the literature of the world, is both public and personal prayer. Some of the poems recite the old mythology of conquering the land. Some tell of the desolations felt by those taken into Babylonian captivity. But nearly all of them are poems of the interior religious experience. None more so than Psalm 139. 'O Lord you have searched me and known me...'

How many religious men and women, since its composition, must have recited this Psalm, with its sense that Yahweh has been with us since our very conception...

> Where can I go from your spirit?
> Or where can I flee from your presence?
> If I ascend to heaven, you are there;
> if I make my bed in Sheol, you are there.
> If I take the wings of the morning
> and settle at the farthest limits of the sea,
> even there your right hand shall lead me,
> and your right hand shall hold me fast. [Psalm 139:7–10]

The psalm appears first to have been written by a religious leader who has been accused of idol-worship. It is an appeal to Yahweh to examine the worshipper, through and through. The preterite in the first verse in most English translations – 'O Lord you have searched me and known me' – is wrong. It is a request to be examined now: 'Yahweh, examine me, and know me yourself!'

Mitchell Dahood SJ renders the final verse as 'Test me and know my cares. Then see if an idol has held sway over me, and lead me into the eternal dominion!'

Does the 'experience' of reading this Psalm constitute an 'experience' of God?

The poem embodies, exemplifies, the transformation of human religious awareness which we associate with the Axial Age. This is

the term generally given to that broad, longish period of history
when Siddhartha Gautama shaved his head and beard and put
on the saffron robe of the Renouncer in the foothills of the
Himalayas, when Socrates was professing that the unexamined
life was not worth living, and when the Hebrew prophets began to
see that true religion is not the mere following of rituals, but the
transformation of the heart. The classic mythological expression
of this transformation, or enlightenment, is Plato's myth, in *The
Republic*, of the Cave, when the initiate, who has been looking at
the flickering of shadows at the back of a cave cast by the fire, and
mistaking this for reality, turns and looks at the light outside the
cave – the true light of the sun.

Whatever the precise date or origin of Psalm 139, it is cognate
with these moments of human enlightenment. What grabs us, in
reading it, is the urgency: the intimacy. A recent translation by
Robert Alter renders the central verses as follows:

> If I take wing with the dawn,
>   if I dwell at the ends of the sea,
> there, too, Your hand leads me,
>   and Your right hand seizes me.
> Should I say, 'Yes, darkness will swathe me,
>   and the night will be light for me,
> Darkness itself will not darken for You,
>   and the night will light up like the day,
>   the dark and the light will be one.
> For You created my innermost parts,
>   wove me in my mother's womb.

Alter reminds us that in fact the Hebrew word here for 'innermost parts' is actually 'kidneys'. (Shades of Leopold Bloom at the beginning of *Ulysses!*) The relationship between the human being who prays and the Living God has been going on since the first mysterious beginnings of the foetus in the womb. Deeper intimacy is not possible. When we pray, it is this profound kinship, this relationship with God which has been there from the beginning of our conception, which we reawaken.

The liturgical, and private, repetition of Psalms since the compilation of the Book in the fourth or fifth century BC has been a – perhaps the – feature of the inner religious life of Judaism, later of Christianity. Every single day, Jews and Christians repeat these poems. In Christian religious houses, the Hours of Prayer are devoted to a recitation of Psalms – not so much in the order printed, but in an order which reflects the patterns of Christian prayer and meditation.

The personal nature of the Psalms, the raw truthfulness of their emotions, is what makes them the enduring prayer book which they have been ever since their composition.

Thomas Merton wrote:

> Of whom can it more truly be said that; 'the word is nigh them, even in their mouth and in their heart' than those who daily recite or chant the Divine Office? If that word is to become for them living and effectual, if it is to penetrate the depths of their interior life and make them contemplatives, they must discover in it the Christ who is the light of the world. He who is the centre of the Old Testament and the New is, above all, the life of the Psalter.

❦

Anyone who has read the Gospel accounts of Jesus's last hours must have been struck by how many phrases from the Scriptures are used in the narrative; and in particular by how many quotations there are from the Old Testament, and in particular from the Psalms.

Let us consider the oldest Gospel, that of Mark. And remember, the Psalms, in Jewish tradition, were the composition of their folk hero, King David, who is supposed to have lived about 1000 BC. In 2 Samuel, we read how King David suffered a rebellion by his son Absalom. He decided to flee his citadel in Jerusalem. Deserted by all but a few followers, he crossed over the Wadi Kidron [2 Samuel 15:23] and went up to pray on the Mount of Olives, weeping as he went. David has lost power. He has become a new type of king, one who must throw himself wholly on the mercy of God. His only power is prayer. It is David the Psalmist who is seen here in the old story, the Psalmist to whom God promised 'Ask of me, and I will make the nations your heritage, and the ends of the earth your possession' [Psalm 2:8] or 'O you who answer prayer! To you all flesh shall come.' [Psalm 65:2].

David's story tells a spiritual message. The legendary founder of Zion, the founder of Jerusalem as the centre of Jewish cultic worship (as opposed to Shechem in the northern kingdom – where this book began), he is in a sense one of the founders of Judaism itself; of that Judaism of which Psalms was the central liturgical text, the main prayer book. In the stories David often behaved badly. The most notable piece of bad behaviour, perhaps, was his stealing the wife of one of his best soldiers, Uriah the Hittite, and sending Uriah into the front line of battle where he would be sure to get himself killed. He was denounced for his behaviour by the prophet Nathan. Furthermore, God punished David and Bathsheba (Uriah's wife) by making their baby die; but their next baby was none other than Solomon himself.

To whatever depths David sank in these stories, however, he always retained his capacity for repentance. He was the type of the Penitent, and in so far as tradition makes him the author of the Psalms, the redactor of the book linked particular Psalms with moments in his life. The penitential Psalm 51, best known to concert-goers in the setting by Monteverdi, is introduced in the Hebrew Bible as 'A Psalm of David, when the prophet Nathan came to him, after he had gone in to Bathsheba'.

David in the Hebrew Bible is therefore both legendary folk hero and type of the Man of Prayer.

Jesus, in Mark's Gospel, had been identified by the blind beggar Bartimaeus as the 'Son of David' [Mark 10:47]. In his disputes with the scribes, Jesus reminded them that they had called the Messiah 'Son of David', even though, in the Psalm, David had written, "'The Lord said to my Lord, 'Sit at my right hand. . .'" David himself calls him Lord; so how can he be his son?', a riposte which Mark tells us delighted a large crowd [Mark 12:36–37]. Mark, in other words, is far along the way to proclaiming, as Matthew and Luke were to do, that Jesus was actually descended from King David. In any event, in the Marcan story of the last two days of Jesus's life, he takes on the Davidic role of the king without followers, weeping on the Mount of Olives. The next day, when he is crucified, Jesus calls out the words of Psalm 22 from the Cross – *Eloi, eloi, lama sabachthani,*

which means, 'My God, my God, why have you forsaken me?'
[Psalm 22:1] 'And someone ran, filled a sponge with sour wine, put it
on a stick, and gave it to him to drink.' [Mark 15:36] Here is another
quotation from the Psalms, this time from Psalm 69, traditionally
associated by Christians with the Crucifixion of Jesus. 'They gave
me poison for food, and for my thirst they gave me vinegar to drink'
[Psalm 69:21].

From that single Psalm, 22, we have, for example, 'All who see me
mock at me' [v.7) and 'They divide out my clothes among themselves,
and for my clothing they cast lots' [v.18].

There can be no doubt that, as in so many other parts of the Bible,
we find here one passage of Scripture being used to provide the
narrative structure for another.

Two very different reasons could be attested for the presence of
these details in the narrative of the Crucifixion. One is that the
soldiers did indeed steal Jesus's clothes and cast lots for them; that
Jesus did indeed cry out 'My God, my God, why have you forsaken
me?' from the Cross, while those who passed by jeered.

Another explanation could be that the Evangelist has used the
Psalm, not as a recollection of anything which actually took place,
but as a meditation on the inner meaning of Christ's death. Jesus
would have prayed in the words of Psalms on a regular basis. Any
Jew (or now, any Christian) brought up in a liturgical tradition
would have much of Psalms by heart; and even those Psalms which
are not literally memorized would have sunk deep into the psyche of
any practising Jew or Christian. So it is perfectly possible that Jesus
himself, for example, cried out words from Psalms as he was dying
on the Cross.

Is it not equally possible, however, that the narrative of the Crucifixion is a literary construct?

Emem, as I was invited to call her, was there to greet me when I arrived at the convent. She was a woman in her early seventies, with short grey hair, a remarkably unlined face, and gardener's hands – the skin at her fingertips was thick and calloused, and although her hands were clean, they had clearly been very recently scrubbed.

—It's good of you to come.

—Kind of you to ask me.

—We did not know who else to contact. And, you see, she did leave this packet for you.

Emem wore a white blouse, a dark blue cardigan and blue slacks. Sandals on bare feet were the only clue as to her calling.

In the 'higher' branches of the Church of England, with which I was more familiar than with the Catholic Church, the remaining nuns still tend to dress like nuns. Emem, I was told later, was an abbreviation for the name she had taken when joining the Order forty-five years before – Sister Margaret Mary of the Sacred Heart.

—We have Mass at midday. You'd be most welcome to join us. It's not going to be a Requiem, but she will be mentioned in the prayers.

—I'd love to be there.

—And do feel free to come to Communion.

—You realize I'm not . . .

—We'd like it – if you feel able to do so. We've all discussed it, and I've squared it with Father Dermot.

—Your chaplain.

She gave a short, rather gruff laugh.

—It's a long time since we had the luxury of a chaplain. There are only four of us now, you see. But Father Dermot comes over as often as he can – he's chaplain at the hospital in Salisbury. And we have another priest we can call on sometimes. But we won't get Mass every day… until one of us is ordained.

We both laughed – though I was not sure why.

By the standards of formal Anglican liturgy, the Mass was remarkably spare. Father Dermot, a pleasant-faced man in his mid-forties, wore simply a white throw-over garment a little like a nightshirt reaching to his ankles, and a coloured stole. He spoke slowly and distinctly. One of the sisters read the first lesson, and Emem read the Epistle and led us in the recitation of the Responsorial Psalm. A third sister, a very small old lady with a melodious voice, read the bidding prayers, which included a commendation of L. to God.

Though it was a simple Eucharist, the priest used the oldest form of Canon available in the new Missal. The Canon of the Mass is the great central prayer of the rite – what in other denominations would be called the Prayer of Consecration. It begins by establishing that the prayer is made in conjunction with all Catholic and Orthodox Christians throughout the world: that is quite a number – well over a fifth of the planet's entire population.

But these millions of people are not the only ones with whom the prayer joins the participants. For there then follows the first of two long catalogues of names of those with whom the worshippers are in communication – the Virgin Mary, the Twelve Apostles, and a list of the early martyrs who died for the faith in the first centuries of Christendom.

The prayer then continues with the central historic claim of Christendom: that, on the night before he suffered, Jesus took bread into his hands, broke the bread, and gave it to his disciples with the words 'This is My Body'; and likewise, when they had eaten, that he gave them the Cup, saying 'This is My Blood'.

The prayer is not over yet, however, for, having commemorated the death, resurrection and ascension of Christ into heaven, the priest prays that the offering will be accepted as the first offerings of Abel in the earliest part of Genesis was accepted; and as the bread and wine offered by the mysterious figure of the High Priest Melchizedek in the story of Abraham. In other words, the Eucharist celebrated here, today, in the twenty-first century, becomes part of an unbroken voice of prayer rising up from the human race since the dawning of humanity itself.

The prayer asks for the dead a place of refreshment, light and peace. And then comes another catalogue of names before gathering all the prayers together: 'Through Him, With Him and In Him. . .'

I did not – do not – understand the thinking behind a 'requiem' mass. I must be too much of a Prot to get my mind around it. How could the celebration of the Communion make God more or less likely to give peace to a departed soul? Surely the Eucharist is the spiritual food of wayfarers on earth, not a bargaining counter? And is there not something presumptuous about thinking that anything we said or thought could affect the destiny of our departed sister? Yet, praying for the dead is another way of loving the dead, and during the recitation of the Mass, I realized how very much I did love L., how much I would miss these strange conversations and disquisitions of hers; I also thought how much of her life had been a secret from me. Were I to research a biography of L., name the small town in New England where she grew up, describe her parents, list her grades, chronicle the graduate work with Frye in Toronto, try to analyse the mental illnesses, ask myself, during all our encounters and non-encounters, whether she wanted a deeper relationship with me – all that is 'archaeology'. She liked reading poetry, but she seldom spoke of fiction. Her sense of the Bible was poetic, not fictive. It did not worry her, as it worried David Friedrich Strauss and George Eliot, that we do not know anything 'about' Elijah, or Jesus or St Paul, in the way that we 'know' the characters in *Middlemarch*. For this reason, I have felt free, in these pages, to mythologize L., to put into her mind, or her letters, words which were in fact spoken by others, and to make her a 'composite' figure, rather as we may suppose that certain New Testament writings were attributed to Paul when in fact they were composed by someone else, or as parables and apothegms in general circulation at the time a particular Gospel was composed were attributed to Jesus.

After the Mass, the nuns gave me a simple meal. It appeared to be a sort of vegetable bake, very dry in texture. Father Dermot did not join us – he drove back into Salisbury. There was no conversation at the meal. One of the sisters read from a biography of Dorothy Day, the American social activist and Catholic convert.

In the small sitting-room afterwards, there was half an hour of recreation in which talking was permitted. There I met Emem's sisters – none of whom was under sixty-five – and they presented me with a brown paper envelope.

—She asked us to give this to you if. . .

On the train back to London, I opened the packet. It was the loose leaves of her 'Bible book', a collection of notebooks and odd pieces of paper which represented a lifetime of thought and work. It is from these notes that the present book is constructed. This is L.'s book as much as mine.

The celebration of the Eucharist, and the use of one of the most ancient prayers of Christendom, spoken quietly, gently, slowly, brought into focus the direction in which my Bible thoughts had been moving. There is no more contemporary, no more popular, way of reading the Bible than in the daily recitation of the liturgy which happens all over the world, in a multitude of languages and a whole variety of situations.

Clearly, as a living witness to the tradition of Bible-steeped Christianity, there is no more obvious or available example. As it happened, I had brought along for train reading the *The Letters of J. R. R. Tolkien*. While he was engaged upon the long task of writing *The Lord of the Rings*, in wartime Oxford, a son was in South Africa serving with the RAF. To this son, Tolkien wrote:

> If you don't do so already, make a habit of the 'praises'. I use them much (in Latin): the Gloria Patri, the Gloria in Excelsis, the Laudate Dominum; the Laudate Pueri Dominum (of which I am specially fond), one of the Sunday psalms; and the Magnificat... If you have these by heart you never need for words of joy. It is also a good and admirable thing to know by heart the Canon of the Mass, for you can

say this in your heart if ever hard circumstance keeps you from hearing Mass.

It would seem that it was a remark by Tolkien to his friend C. S. Lewis which played a decisive role in the conversion of Lewis from theism to specific Christian belief. Nothing could illustrate more purely the dilemma I had reached in my journey around the Bible. Clearly, from all I had learned, reading about the Bible, it is mythology. As Frye had written, 'Man lives, not directly or nakedly in nature like the animals, but within a mythological universe, a body of assumptions and beliefs developed from his existential concerns'.

To demythologize the Bible is to destroy it, as Frye says elsewhere.

But does it make any difference to our appreciation of the Bible whether we are happy to live in the protection of its mythological wings without asking the question of whether any of it is, objectively speaking, verifiable, let alone 'true'?

At the centre of the Mass which I had heard in the convent was an historical assertion. 'The night before he was betrayed, he took bread.'

The central Christian act of worship supposedly goes back in an unbroken line to the person of Jesus himself. Clearly, the lives of the nuns I had just visited were fed and nourished by the Mass. For millions upon millions of human beings since AD 50 or so, when Paul described the Eucharist in Corinth, this rite has been enacted, and people have felt in it that they knew the presence of Christ. It is the centre of Christian life, and of its tradition. This action – taking bread, breaking it, repeating the words of Jesus, 'This is My Body'

– is something which Christians have been doing as long as there have been Christians.

That is a matter of fact.

Is there any need to go beyond this fact to establish facts which are not known – such as whether Jesus really did institute the Meal? And if so, do we need to know when he did so?

Clearly, the Meal, the Eucharist, is part of the very earliest tradition. For a practising Christian, therefore, who takes the tradition seriously, it is part of the faith, not merely that Christians have been doing this since, say, AD 50, but that it is a rite instituted by the Lord.

> For I received from the Lord what I also handed on to you, that the Lord Jesus on the night when he was betrayed took a loaf of bread, and when he had given thanks, he broke it and said, 'This is my body that is for you. Do this in remembrance of me.' In the same way he took the cup also, after supper, saying, 'This cup is the new covenant in my blood. Do this as often as you drink it, in remembrance of me.' For as often as you eat this bread and drink the cup, you proclaim the Lord's death until he comes. [1 Corinthians 11:23–26]

It might be supposed that this is an historical statement, and it is therefore either 'true' or 'untrue'. Unfortunately, things are not as simple as that. Only by continuing to think in an 'imaginative' or 'mythological' way will we make any progress in understanding the historical origins of the Eucharist.

Two things might not be obvious when we first approach the matter, and it might be worth stating them baldly. One is a piece of theology. The other is a piece of history, or rather, of non-history.

The theology first. The first Eucharist was not the Last Supper. The first Eucharist, for Christians, was the Crucifixion. The Last Supper – whenever it took place – and if you believe it took place – was an exposition of the theology of the Cross. Jesus took bread, broke it, as his body would be broken; he said, 'Do this in remembrance of me'. The Eucharist was left to his first followers as the everlasting remembrance of, and re-enactment of, his act of self-giving on the Cross. The Eucharist is not just a 'let's pretend' version of the Last Supper. It is what was called in the old pagan religions, and what is still called by Christians, a Mystery, a solemn symbol which leads us into the heart of what faith believes happened on the Cross. It therefore takes us, absolutely immediately, beyond any question where 'Did it or did it not happen?' could ever be answered by any known criterion.

Secondly, the history, or rather the non-history. The Gospels cannot be used as historical evidence, one way or the other, for the question of Eucharistic origin. They were written down by and for Christian communities for whom the Eucharist was already the centre of their life and worship. As well as recording the Lord's words 'on the night when he was betrayed', Paul also saw the sacrifice of Jesus on the Cross as a Passover. Reading the Exodus story typologically, as so many Jews did – I was tempted to write, as *all* Jews of this time did – he applies the story of the first Passover to the story of Jesus's death. In common with all Jews, Paul kept Pesach, or Passover, ate the Lamb, which had been ritually sacrificed in the Temple in remembrance of the Jewish deliverance from Egypt, as an emblem or token of human redemption from sin. Paul saw the death of Jesus as the new Passover. 'For our paschal lamb, Christ, has been sacrificed. Therefore, let us celebrate the festival, not with the old yeast, the yeast of malice and evil, but with the unleavened bread of sincerity and truth.' [1 Corinthians 5:7–8]

Paul did not say that Jesus took the loaf, and spoke the words of the Eucharist at Passover. He said Jesus was the true Passover Lamb, and then, in another place, a little later he said that Jesus was betrayed the day after the Supper. Pass a whole generation and the two metaphors have become embedded into Christian tradition. Jesus the Paschal Lamb is offered in the Holy Sacrifice of the Eucharist. The Eucharist was instituted at Passover-time. But although that is what came to be written down in the period AD 70–100, by the Gospel writers, *it is not the earliest tradition.*

The Gospel writers wrote down their accounts of the Supper, thereby landing later historians with a real conundrum. Matthew, Mark and Luke all want to make the Supper into a Passover meal. There are many people who firmly believe that the Supper had to have been a Passover meal, or it would somehow lose its authenticity. The trouble with this is twofold. It asks us to believe – if we believe the earliest testimony that Jesus established the Supper the night when he was betrayed – that Jesus was arrested at Passover, and that the Jewish High Priests, their entourage of acolytes and their Sanhedrin, their court, were all in full session during the most sacred period of the Jewish year, to decide the question of whether to hand over to the Romans for crucifixion either Jesus or a man called Barabbas who 'was in prison with the rebels who had committed murder during the insurrection' [Mark 15:7]. Even if you believed that the High Priest was prepared to suspend the Feast of

Pesach for the sake of Jesus – his high profile as a troublemaker, or his supposed blasphemies against Judaism making it necessary to deal with him as soon as possible – why would they have cancelled Pesach just for Barabbas? It does not make any sense at all.

If you persist in thinking that Jesus died around Passover time, then the Fourth Gospel makes much better historical sense, and much deeper theological sense too. This describes the Supper happening during the period of preparation for Pesach. Jesus dies on the Cross, in this version, while the Passover lambs are being slaughtered in the Temple. On the other hand, note well that the Fourth Gospel does not have the institution of the Eucharist occurring at the Supper. On the contrary. It has its long disquisition on the Eucharist in its sixth chapter, while Jesus was still in Galilee. It follows the great Sign of the Feeding which is obviously seen as symbolic of the Eucharist by this author.

Either way, you are not going to be able to get any historical facts out of the Gospels on this matter. This is not because the Gospels are being sneaky, or trying to trick us. It is because they are so convinced by the two imaginative truths about Jesus promulgated by Paul – that Jesus is our Passover Lamb, and that Jesus left us the Supper as a token of his presence – that they do not trouble themselves to write history in the post-Enlightenment sense *at all*.

The conundrum of whether the Eucharist was instituted by Jesus, and if so when, throws into the sharpest relief the bigger question, of whether the New Testament gives us anything like historical 'evidence' for the faith.

Two recent books illustrate quite different answers to the matter. They are *The Mystery of the Last Supper* by Colin J. Humphreys and

Beyond the Quest for the Historical Jesus: Memoir of a Discovery by Thomas L. Brodie. Both are densely worked books, so that I mention them partly in order to apologize to their authors, since there is not room, in a book of this kind, to summarize all the intricacies of their arguments.

Sir Colin Humphreys is Professor and Director of Research at the Department of Materials Science and Metallurgy at the University of Cambridge; as a second string to his distinguished bow, he has entered the (mine)field of Biblical history. He believes himself to have reconstructed the exact date of the Crucifixion. He gets over the difficulty of it having occurred during the Jewish Passover by claiming that Jesus followed a slightly different calendar, namely that which was discovered among the Caves of Qumran in 1948 (the Dead Sea Scrolls). In this, Sir Colin is following the lead of Pope Benedict XVI who also thought that Jesus followed the Qumran calendar. This would place the events of that last week a few days earlier, assuming that the first century Jewish calendar can be calculated with this degree of accuracy. Sir Colin carries a table detailing 'the effect of a cloudy sky delaying the date of Nisan 14 in Jerusalem, AD 26–36'.

Sir Colin's theory is interesting *as a theory*. It is hard to see why or how it could affect the state of mind of any Christian preparing to attend a celebration of the Eucharist. For any such person, the reality would be the living presence of Christ in the broken bread, in the shared chalice. This incomprehensible Mystery could not depend upon whether Jesus followed the Qumran or the mainstream Jewish calendar for the keeping of 14th Nisan.

The tradition is of Christ present in the Church, present in the

Eucharist, present in the hearts of the faithful. Part of that tradition is that the Meal owes its origin to Jesus himself, but we are not bound to think of the Mass as taking its origin in a particular Passover meal. On the contrary, the symbolism of the Passover meal, to which the Eucharist owes much, draws not on the dating of the Last Supper, but on Paul's idea of Christ as our Paschal Lamb.

So, Colin Humphreys' approach seems to me like historical hobbyism, what L. called archaeology. At the beginning of his book, he quotes Richard Dawkins as saying, 'The only difference between *The Da Vinci Code* and the gospels is that the gospels are ancient fiction while *The Da Vinci Code* is modern fiction'. Humphreys thinks to refute this sentence by establishing the 'historical' evidence for the exact week in which the Last Supper took place. It is done with the best intentions, of course, but is it not playing into the hands of materialism to make everything depend upon the plausibility of a theory put forward by one retired scientist about weather conditions and calendars in ancient Palestine?

Is not a more powerful answer to Dawkins's claim, that he has made a 'category mistake'? 'Fiction' can mean many things, evidently. Dan Brown's book is a fast-paced piece of thriller writing based upon crackpot theories concerning the Knights Templar, secret codes in Leonardo da Vinci and the unhistorical story that Jesus was secretly married to Mary Magdalen. The Gospels are not 'fiction' in this sense. They are not written as stories which the authors knew to be untrue. They use typological devices – fictive devices, if you will – to convey deep theological and spiritual truths. The truths which these mythologies convey have inspired some of the most heroic lives, some of the most stupendous buildings, some of the most glorious works of music and art in the world's history. When Dan Brown's book has come close to doing the same, then Dawkins's comparison will stand, but until there is an oratorio of *The Da Vinci Code* to match Bach's *St Matthew Passion*, or a Dan Brown Memorial Building to match Canterbury Cathedral, we can continue to go to church without too much fear that we are merely believing 'fiction'.

Or can we? Although Dawkins and Humphreys both display a certain woodenness of approach – indeed, a complete lack of imagination, if one is being candid – how would it be if the characters and events of the New Testament were in fact entirely invented – fiction in the sense Dawkins and Humphreys meant? This is the view put forward by the Roman Catholic friar Thomas Brodie OP in *Beyond the Quest for the Historical Jesus*.

Brodie has spent a lifetime researching the typology of the Bible. Towards the end of his book, he writes:

> Insofar as the figure of Christ engages sin, death, and resurrection, it is a reminder, first of all, that reality challenges every human being to face squarely into suffering and death. There is no easy road. Life has more suffering not only than we want but often even than we imagine. Yet the figure of Christ is also a reminder, amid all the world's pains, that the heart of reality is a compassion that knows us through and through, and that there is more life in heaven and on earth than many of us ever dream of. . .

Brodie's writings are an attractive blend of scholarship, intellectual inquiry, and an imaginative, even poetic, 'take' upon the world. Like many Biblical scholars, he has travelled a long way, in his own journey of faith, from the days when he joined the Order of Preachers as a young novice. In fact, he has decided that Jesus did not exist. 'The tragedy with the quest for the historical Jesus is not just that it is seeking something impossible – but that – somewhat as Dawkins reduces the mind – the historical reconstructions present forms of Jesus that are desperately reduced. . . The quest for the historical Jesus installs the flicker of a matchstick in place of the aurora borealis. . .'

I can imagine L. responding positively to that sentence: I can imagine, likewise, Brodie's great Dominican predecessor, Thomas Aquinas, agreeing. What is Aquinas's great Eucharistic hymn except an acknowledgement that Christ remains eternally hidden, and eternally to be worshipped, behind Symbol?

> *Plagas, sicut Thomas, non intueor;*
> *Deum tamen meum te Confiteor.*

I do not see the wounds, as Thomas did, yet I confess you to be my God.

But Brodie, in the tradition of what was once called Catholic Modernism, goes much further than Aquinas. He actually believes that Jesus is a literary construct. He believes the same, too, of Paul. The imaginative advantage of Brodie's theory is that it is non-reductionist. It does not wish to demolish the whole rich tradition of Christendom and replace it with arid 'archaeology'. On the contrary, he rejoices in all the imaginative possibilities of faith in Christ. The theology of Cardinal Newman, the poetry of George Herbert, the great traditions of inner prayer in religious houses, the music and the buildings inspired by Christianity remain intact. It is simply that, as we go back, and back and back in the tradition, all we find, in Brodie's version, is an elaborate series of literary types. He rejects any notion of an oral tradition antedating the literary constructs of the New Testament texts. Where is the evidence for such a tradition? No, all we have is the written text. And 'in testing the Gospels, essentially every strand concerning the life of Jesus consistently yielded clear signs of being dependent on older writings'.

I am sure this is broadly true. Brodie has spent most of a longish professional life establishing its truth. When Mary sings her hymn of praise to God, known as the Magnificat [Luke 1:46 ff], the words are largely drawn from Hannah's Prayer in the First Book of Samuel [1 Samuel 2:1–10]. When the disciples receive the prophetic call to follow Christ and are told that the Son of Man has nowhere to lay his head [Luke 9:57–62], it is a close parallel to the call of the Prophet Elijah in the wilderness [1 Kings 19:4–21] and so on, over and over again.

There is a great attractiveness about Brodie's book – to me at any rate. Did not Paul, or – if you follow Brodie – 'Paul', or whoever wrote the Letter to the Colossians – write, 'So if you have been raised with Christ, seek the things that are above, where Christ is, seated at the right hand of God. Set your minds on things that are above, not on things that are on earth, for you have died and your life is hidden with Christ in God'? [Colossians 3:1–3] Would it not be something of a relief to abandon all the pointless 'archaeology' of worry about whether the Bible is historically true, and concentrate upon living a spiritual life, drawing upon all the riches of prayer to be found in its pages, especially in Psalms and the Gospels?

'To say Jesus did not exist as a historical individual does not mean he has been eliminated. Copernicus did not eliminate the earth. He simply saw it in a new way,' writes Brodie.

What is remarkable about Brodie's thesis is that, in many respects, it does not alter the way in which most Christians could still go on leading rich inner lives, fed by sacrament and Scripture, whether the historical Jesus had existed or not. This has been realized at least since the Abbé Loisy wrote *L'Evangile et l'Eglise* in 1902.

Earlier critics of the New Testament, including those intent on proving it to be historically true, have tended to take it to bits, akin to those 'restorers' of antique sculpture who remove later accretions and would prefer a few heaps of disconnected limbs which authentically dated from the second century BC, rather than a finished statue, whose arms, nose and ears had been added by a restorer in Roman times or in the sixteenth century. The beauty of the Modernist approach to the Bible is that it leaves the artefact intact. Brodie quotes with approval an exchange at a Biblical conference when the Marriage Feast of Cana was being discussed. 'Did it really happen?' 'What a European question! In Asia, they would ask, "What does it mean?"'

Brodie and scholars like him have done so much to enable us to read the Bible with new eyes: by making us see the kind of books which compose the Bible. In so doing, Brodie has worked himself into a position where the books are all that he can see. In those books, he can see infinite riches of symbolism and spiritual strength. But is there in the end something unsatisfactory about his theory? He has analysed the way in which the Biblical writings are put together, with repeated cross-reference and typological reading of earlier texts. But although the New Testament writers write about Jesus in a mythological way, does this entitle us to think this is all they were doing – rather than writing a myth which happened to be true? If the neatness of Brodie's thesis is what ultimately leaves our curiosity unsatisfied, can we derive any answer to the inevitable question – Did It Really Happen?

SEVEN

THE REBIRTH
OF IMAGES

But the whole Bible, not its prophetical portions only, is written on the principle of development. As the Revelation proceeds, it is ever new, yet ever old.

John Henry Newman, *An Essay on the*
Development of Christian Doctrine

WE HAVE PASSED through six parts of our seven-part journey. In the first part, on an abortive visit to Mount Gerizim and the ancient shrine of Shechem, we learnt of the aridity of the dead-end Quest for the Historical Jesus detached from the Christ of traditional faith. Jesus was seen from the beginning through the prism of pre-existent Biblical metaphors – as the 'living water' written about by Jeremiah [2:13, 17:13], and as the sacrificial lamb of Pesach, the high point in the Jewish liturgical year. The people who wrote the Bible by and large had this typological way of reading the Bible and it would be fiendishly difficult, if not impossible, to disentangle the historical 'nuggets' which their method of writing might have contained.

One thing which has been with us from the beginning is a consciousness, not always apparent in academic books about the Bible, nor in books written with the specific apologetic purpose of converting the reader to particular forms of literalism, that the Bible has not had a life detached from people.

It did not appear, as some have been persuaded, that the Book of Mormon appeared all in one go, dictated by an Archangel. 'Fundamentalists' want to make the true, organic, living Bible into an ersatz Bible like the Book of Mormon. But the real Bible was the creation of many writers and – just as important – many trans-lators, and – even more important – many readers who soaked it up, reading it daily until it became part of their lives, and until their lives became part of *it*.

It has not only dictated the way men and women have thought about their place in the scheme of things. It has itself been shaped by what they thought, experienced, felt. So, with perhaps the most basic religious question of all – is there a God? – the Bible begins with surprising answers. Most of what human beings have taken for gods, or religions, are utterly rejected, over and over again, by the Bible. The Torah proposes a totally new way of looking at God. Indeed, by the time the earliest Bible-writers were putting together the stories, laws and ordinances which make up the first books of the Bible, they had decided that there were no gods at all.

The Bible God is therefore different entirely in kind from previous conceptions of God, though it bears points of resemblance to (roughly) contemporary rejections of the gods by Plato and the Buddha.

'You shall have no other gods before me'[Exodus 20:3]. It is a text which is at the basis of the Judaeo-Christian inheritance. It seems on the face of it belligerent, intolerant, even foolish. By what right do the People of the Book claim that they have all the answers, and that those who do not share their beliefs should be cast into outer darkness? But this is not what these words, written by P in whenever it was (500–200 BC), really mean. Belligerent, intolerant people have seized on the words to mean that We are Right and They are Wrong. But the words really mean: banish all preconceptions about religion from your mind. Get rid of them. Banish idols from your mind. If you are making the God of the Bible into an idol, banish him too. If you are making the Bible an idol, banish that.

God is a Verb. That is the message of the Pentateuch. God is emergent, God is not a being within the established order, he is being. All depends on him, not the other way around. That lies at the heart of the first perception of the Bible in the Torah.

In the Prophets, we began to see the difference between the worship of an idol and the true worship of One who is a Verb. For the worship of Yahweh transforms life, undermines preju-dices, upsets hierarchies. The Prophet is the archetypical figure who troubles Israel; that is, who troubles kings and authorities and upsets preconceptions. While the secularized intelligentsia in the West had decided that the Bible was a dead letter, we contem-plated the lives of those for whom the Bible was a living Word – Dr King's leadership of the Civil Rights Movement, Father Huddleston's campaigns against apartheid in South Africa and

Solzhenitsyn's determination, if necessary single-handedly, to tell the truth about Stalin's Soviet Union were all directly inspired by the spirit of Scriptural Prophecy. 'Rejoice, and be exceeding glad: for great is your reward in heaven: for so persecuted they the prophets which were before you' [Matthew 5:12 AV].

The third great section of the Bible which we considered was that known as the Writings. As we did so, we contemplated the meaning of the word 'Wisdom' in its Christian history. Building the Hagia Sophia was a way of 'reading the Bible'. Architecture, painting, music and the exercise of the imagination – these were all the activities of those who found in the Bible an inspiration to follow the God who is a Verb.

In Chapters Five and Six, we considered two Wisdom books in greater depth. Job is one of the greatest works of literature in the world, a tragedy of Sophoclean or Shakespearean dimensions. It is the Bible in miniature. It is deeply subversive of any pietistic or contentedly 'religious' view of the world. It appears to be a story about God testing a man, but it is in truth a story about humanity putting God on trial, as the Rabbis put God on trial in Auschwitz. (When they'd found him guilty, they went to their prayers, an exact parallel to Job's cry, 'Though he slay me, yet will I trust in him' [Job 13:15 AV].)

Out of Job – the perfect man both embodying the Divine Wisdom and putting the Divine Judge on trial – comes Christian theology and an understanding of the Cross.

The other great Wisdom book, which has been the prayer book of synagogues and churches for, probably, two and a half thousand years, is Psalms. These poems are the poems of the inner life of humanity; in them, humanity has brought its exultant joy at the presence and goodness of God, its self-disgust at human wrong-doing, its anguished fear of death, its desolated sense of God's absence.

The book of Psalms has been at the centre of Christian piety since the beginning. Not only monks and nuns and priests, but all Christian people have used the repetition of the Psalms as a template off which to read their own backslidings, triumphs, griefs, doubts... Many of the Psalms, as with other texts of the Old Testament, have been used by the Gospel-writers to shape the story of Jesus, and especially the stories of his death.

But here we confronted a difficulty. We understand something of what the Christian life is, in all its spiritual richness, and all its potential for good. But if all the texts of the Gospels are really a tapestry of quotations from the Old Testament, if Jesus is constantly made by the authors of the Gospels to correspond to tropes and types from the old Bible, how do we know that he is any more than those tropes and types? Is there not a case for believing that he never in fact existed?

And here we move to our seventh and final stage of the journey.

L.'s letters and conversations about the Bible, over a period of three decades, persuaded me of the attractiveness, and the interest, of the Biblical texts. But the conversation was interrupted by her death. Several years passed during which I wrote books which had nothing to do with the Bible – some novels, some works of modern history. I had started to read the Bible again, however, and to read it in (to me) new ways. I found myself wondering whether I was qualified to write the most difficult part of the story – namely the chapter about the New Testament. It would be a chapter which had to decide the plausibility of the New Testament as an historical witness.

The New Testament is made up of twenty-seven pieces of writing, dating from around AD 50 to, perhaps, 100. During this half-century, the very word 'Witness' to the burgeoning Christian Church took on differing depths of meaning. Christians 'witnessed' to their faith in the most costly way of all, a fact attested by our use of the Greek word for witness: martyr. In what amounts to a Fifth Gospel, the Roman Canon, which I had heard in the nuns' chapel, the story does not simply revolve around a recollection of Jesus and his twelve; it recites the names of martyrs, those who were prepared to die, often in the most extreme agony, rather than deny the Gospel.

How does one go about trying to build a satisfactory picture of the New Testament and its world? To put it another way, what can a modern historian, or interested inquirer, get out of these twenty-seven texts? Those who believe that it is possible to make a Quest for the Historical Jesus, of the kind I so vainly attempted in my book and TV film in Chapter One, would of course look for the earliest known references to Jesus, and start from there. They would try to 'deconstruct' the Gospels for nuggets of what might – perhaps – be plausible pieces of historical 'evidence'.

But the Gospels do not yield up much in the way of historical evidence. If we are wishing to ask historical questions about the New Testament, it might be better to concentrate on something which we know to be an historical event: namely, that great historical event which had so explosive, catastrophic an effect upon Judaism and upon Christianity: namely the destruction of Jerusalem in AD 70. If we chose one New Testament text which dated before the destruction of the city and the Temple, and one text which dated from after that event, what results would that yield?

I'm going to start my exploration with an obviously non-historical text – the Letter to the Hebrews. We do not look here for dateable events, but for concepts, ideas, images to nourish and inform the mind. In so far as they provide us with 'evidence' or 'witnesses', it is not evidence about Jesus but, rather, evidence of what the men and women of this turbulent time believed about Jesus.

Although Hebrews is called a Letter, it is really more of a treatise. We do not know who wrote it. The author's attitude to the Old Testament texts has much in common with that of the Jews of Alexandria, but this does not locate the treatise definitively. The author clearly wrote as if the full, complicated pattern of the liturgical year in the Temple, with all its observances and rituals, was in full swing. Had the Temple been a heap of ruins, he would surely have stated that this was the case, since it would have, tragically, so fitted his purpose: namely to demonstrate that the old faith had been supplanted by the death of Christ and his passing into the heavens as our true High Priest. So Hebrews is pre-AD 70 – one of the earliest New Testament books after the writings of Paul.

Hebrews has two beliefs in common with all the other New Testament texts: the belief that they were living at the end of time [Hebrews 1:2] and the belief that the Jewish religion, with all its longevity, its wealth of tradition, its past, was no more than a preparation for the coming of Jesus. Whereas the previous 'witnesses' of

Jewish history existed in the world of literal history, Jesus had taken his followers out of story and ritual into the Truth itself. The author is clearly a Platonist of sorts who believes that what we see in this world is a shadow of the reality in heaven. But he focuses this view on the figure of Jesus: 'Therefore, since we are surrounded by so great a cloud of witnesses, let us also lay aside every weight and the sin that clings so closely, and let us run with perseverance the race that is set before us, looking to Jesus the pioneer and perfecter of our faith, who for the sake of the joy that was set before him endured the cross, disregarding its shame, and has taken his seat at the right hand of the throne of God' [Hebrews 12:1–2].

The author tells us, then, that Jesus died on a cross, and that he is now in heaven. Moreover, the author sees the death of Jesus as the true reality, of which all the ceremonies in the Temple had only been foreshadowings. For, as the High Priest and his acolytes year by year offered sacrifices for sin, and entered in and out of the Holy of Holies, so now Jesus, our true High Priest, has died for our sins, washed us of our sins once and for all, and entered into the true Holy of Holies, namely heaven. The ritual formalism of Judaism and all its liturgical and scriptural tradition have merely been leading to this one temporal pivot, the death of Jesus on the Cross.

Had we been present at any crucifixion, including that of Jesus (and on one occasion Pontius Pilate had over two thousand Jews crucified), we would have seen a day-long humiliating torture in which a human being, whose flesh had been torn in wrists and ankles, was nailed to a wooden cross, dying eventually from asphyxiation. It is hard to imagine a more horrible death, nor one in which the dying person was more degraded. Yet early Christianity insisted upon seeing this appalling torture as a triumph by a victorious Christ. 'Therefore, my friends, since we have confidence to enter the sanctuary by the blood of Jesus, by the new and living way that he opened for us through the curtain (that is, through his flesh), and since we have a great priest over the house of God, let us approach with a true heart in full assurance of faith, with our hearts sprinkled clean from an evil conscience and our bodies washed with pure water.' [Hebrews 10:19–22]

The author shares this view with Paul, who is our earliest Christian witness. Paul, who was an observant Jew who had originally been hostile to the Christian movement, had a blinding Apocalypse or Revelation which convinced him that Jesus, who had been crucified, was alive [Galatians 1:12]. Paul saw the death of Jesus as having done away forever with the entire Jewish Torah. Whereas in the past, humanity looked to save itself by slavishly following the moral code set forth in the Law, freedom was now poured out by God through the saving act of the Crucifixion. Through this disgraceful criminal death, humanity itself, Jews and Gentiles alike, is set free. 'May I never boast of anything except the cross of our Lord Jesus Christ, by which the world has been crucified to me, and I to the world. For neither circumcision nor uncircumcision is anything; but a new creation is everything!' [Galatians 6:14–15]

Paul told his Galatian converts (in modern-day Ankara) that his Apocalypse occurred some twenty years before he wrote the letter – which is dateable to around AD 50–51. In other words, his experience of a revelation of the risen Christ would have occurred soon after the actual Crucifixion of Jesus.

It is sometimes said, or supposed, that we have no evidence between the supposed date of the Crucifixion (AD 30–33?) and the writing down of the Gospels post-AD 70. But Paul's Letter to the Galatians is an account of a visionary experience of Christ which took place very soon after the Crucifixion. His revolutionary interpretation of the meaning of Jesus's death, had, he recalled twenty years later, scandalized his fellow Jews, even those who counted themselves as followers of Jesus. But lest it be supposed that Paul is worshipping a 'Christ' of his own invention, with no connection with the earthly, historical Jesus – whom many people in the years AD 50–55 could clearly remember – he makes allusion to the historical Jesus. For example, in his letters to the converts at Corinth, Paul alludes to the fact that the historical Jesus instituted the Supper, the Christian Sacrament, and that he forbade the remarriage of the divorced.

The earliest records of what men and women thought about Jesus, then, are not quite what you would expect. They are not memories of a simple teacher and healer. Rather, they are beliefs about his death on a cross – which must in reality have been a sordid, and pathetic sight, as crucifixion always was – as the key, saving moment of human history.

And, as for Hebrews, so in the earliest writings, there is a belief that Jesus pleads for us at the right hand of God. Writing to the Christians at Philippi from prison (perhaps from Rome in about AD 60?) Paul quotes a hymn:

Let the same mind be in you that was in Jesus Christ, who, though he was in the form of God, did not regard equality with God as something to be exploited, but emptied himself,

taking the form of a slave, being born in human likeness.
And being found in human form, he humbled himself and
became obedient to the point of death – even death on a
cross. Therefore God also highly exalted him and gave him
the name that is above every name, so that at the name of
Jesus every knee should bend, in heaven and on earth and
under the earth, and every tongue should confess that Jesus
Christ is Lord, to the glory of God the Father. [Philippians
2:5–11]

This was the early testimony of what his followers believed about
Jesus. How could anyone believe this about an earthly man, who was
still remembered, and whose family were still the leading members of
the Jerusalem church? One answer which we have already considered
is that this early Church, this group of visionary Jews, created a type
of the ideal Messiah; made up an image of suffering Judaism under
the Roman tyranny; constructed from Scriptural texts a figure like
the Suffering Servant in Isaiah, like the patient Job, like the ritual
Priests of the Temple, and the Sacrificial Lambs which they were
killing each Passover-time. If this is what these first Christians did,
it was an extraordinarily complex and ingenious work of collective
imagination, for all the evidence suggests that a far-flung group
of people were involved in the exercise – Paul, or, if you think he
was also an invented construct, the School of 'Paul', writing in Asia
Minor, Macedonia and Greece; Mark, probably constructing a
Gospel in Rome; the Johannine School (possibly in Ephesus); the
Jerusalem Church; and the author of Hebrews – all very different,
all giving pictures of Jesus which differ, and even contradict one

another in certain details, but all agreed on the story of his bodily resurrection and his power, through his death and resurrection and return to his Heavenly Father, to save us from our sins.

Stop reading for a moment and just consider what the spare – very spare – 'evidence' of the New Testament is telling us. It tells us that believers in Jesus Christ, stretching right back to the time of his death, were not holding him in their memory as the pacifist prophet imagined by Tolstoy or Ernest Renan. On the contrary. They sought the language of Scripture, poetry, symbol to express the belief that Jesus, hideously tortured and crucified by the Romans, had died, been buried and risen again.

The fact that they expressed these beliefs does not prove that the Resurrection actually happened.

The New Testament documents are only a testimony of what the early Christians believed. They produce no 'evidence' of the kind we should look for in a law court. But we are entitled to ask those who take the view that the documents are purely literary constructs, *why* any group of human beings would have invented this particular set of letters, Gospel narratives, hymns, apocalyptic visions? And, having invented them, be prepared to suffer and to die for them? I am not sufficiently imaginative to see how a group of writers sat down and decided to write, over a period of about forty years, a set of nearly thirty books which were a sort of exercise in literary 'construction', piecing together pictures of an imagined Jesus from Old Testament quotations. . . Clearly, one explanation is that they could have done so because Paul was deluded, in his original Apocalypse, but wrote and spoke about it so inspiringly that he convinced others. But Paul wrote of those who had adopted the faith of Jesus a good fourteen years before he ever met them: these were the Jerusalem Christians with whom he violently quarrelled, over the question of whether followers of Jesus should continue to keep the Jewish dietary laws and practise circumcision.

To the Corinthians [1 Corinthians 15:6], Paul claimed that, after the Resurrection, over five hundred witnesses in Jerusalem saw Christ. It is a problematic assertion, since no such multitude is recorded in any of the Gospels, but it is one of the earliest 'witness statements' about the Resurrection.

There have been any number of books of what L. would no doubt have called 'archaeology', trying to establish that the Resurrection actually took place. They have titles like *Who Moved the Stone?* No doubt such books were written with admirable intentions, but the Bible is not such a book. In the Fourth Gospel, there is the story of Doubting Thomas. When Jesus had appeared to the disciples, who were locked in an upper room a week after his death, Thomas (who was called the Twin) was not with them. When he heard of Jesus's appearance, he refused to believe it.

A week later his disciples were again in the house, and Thomas was with them. Although the doors were shut, Jesus came and stood among them and said, 'Peace be with you.' Then he said to Thomas, 'Put your finger here and see my hands. Reach out your hand and put it in my side. Do not doubt but believe.' Thomas answered him, 'My Lord and my God!' Jesus said to him, 'Have you believed because you have

seen me? Blessed are those who have not seen and yet have
come to believe.' [John 20:26–29]

The remarkable thing about this particular narrative is that it
is the exact opposite of archaeological attempts to 'prove' the
Resurrection. It says that those first witnesses were indeed witnesses
to a stupendous event. But it was more blessed to belong to the later
generations, who had not seen, but had begun to grasp the significance of the Christian faith. A similar point is made by Luke, in his
story of the two men walking to a village called Emmaus, downcast
after Jesus's death. They were joined by a third with whom they
talked of the sad events leading up to the Crucifixion.

Only when they entered their lodgings and turned in for the
evening, and when the stranger made to leave them, did they ask
him to join them. 'When he was at the table with them, he took
bread, blessed and broke it, and gave it to them. Then their eyes were
opened, and they recognized him' [Luke 24:30–31].

In both Gospels, they are not downplaying the astonishing
physical fact of the Resurrection. They are not saying that it was
something which had only happened in the imagination or in a
spiritual sense. But in both cases, what was even more important
than the first dawning wonder of the Resurrection itself was the
continuing faith of the Church. The stranger, whom they so
unaccountably had not recognized in the roadside, is known to the
faithful in the breaking of bread.

What's wrong with the idea of Jesus as a purely literary construct? Two things.

First, the messiness of the documentary evidence. Not *all* the texts fit into a previous Hebrew template, not every moment of the Gospels is a *midrash* on older scripture – though an amazing number are.

Take the earliest Gospel, perhaps written down forty years after the events it describes – perhaps in Rome. If you believe that it is an elaborate literary construct without any reference to history, then one of the most remarkable things about it is the ingenuity with which it gives names to even minor characters.

As we have already observed, there is no doubt that Mark – in common with most New Testament writers – places the story within a pre-existent Old Testament trope. So, we have read of Jesus, Son of David, following the exact pattern of the older story of King David, who, deserted by his followers, climbs the Mount of Olives in tears.

But then there is the story, a little later on, of Peter's denial. Peter sat in the courtyard of the High Priest, warming himself by the fire, while Jesus was being interrogated within. And one of the servant girls remarked that she recognized him. He was one of the followers of Jesus. Peter denied it hotly. The assertion is repeated, and so is the denial. 'Then after a little while the bystanders again said to Peter, "Certainly you are one of them; for you are a Galilean." But he began to curse, and he swore an oath, "I do not know this man you are talking about." At that moment the cock crowed for the second time. Then Peter remembered that Jesus had said to him, "Before the cock crows twice, you will deny me three times." And he broke down and wept.' [Mark 14:70–72]

As well as being very moving, this passage is of great literary interest. Erich Auerbach, in his classic work *Mimesis: The Representation of Reality in Western Literature*, writes, 'A scene like Peter's denial fits into no antique genre. It is too serious for comedy, too contemporary and everyday for tragedy, politically too insignificant for history – and the form which was given it is one of such immediacy that its like does not exist in the literature of antiquity.'

Auerbach's magisterial book reminds us that the Bible was not alone in following known tropes, building up 'new' books by means of either imitating old ones, or in effect scissors and pasting. And this method of writing would go on right through the Middle Ages. Suetonius, writing *The Lives of the Twelve Caesars*, borrowed from the lives of Greek heroes. Likewise, when Einhard, in the ninth century, wanted to make Charlemagne seem Imperial, he borrowed chunks of Suetonius to describe him; and when Asser, some years later, wanted to write a book about Alfred the Great, he lifted whole phrases and anecdotes from Einhard. This makes it difficult to pin down the accuracy of the stories in any of these books, but no one for that reason supposes that the Twelve Caesars or Charlemagne or Alfred the Great were just literary constructs, still less that they did not exist. It was because they did exist, and were considered important, that the authors chose to dignify them in this particular way of writing.

The Gospels, which follow this practice, also contain material which is unlike this. Peter's denial is only one example. Consider the moment later when Jesus, staggering under the weight of the Cross, which he is forced to carry to the place of execution, needs help: 'they led him out to crucify him. They compelled a passer-by, who was coming in from the country, to carry his cross; it was Simon of Cyrene, the father of Alexander and Rufus.' [Mark 15:20–21]

It is hard to think of reasons why the author should have written these sentences in a book which is just a 'construct' of fictitious events. You could say he did so with deliberate intent to deceive, to add plausibility; that he was a strange mixture of, on the one hand, a creator of tropes – such as Jesus on the Mount of Olives – and a realist who added the details of Peter's denial, or the name of the man helping to carry the cross to add plausibility.

But this in itself seems an inherently implausible thing to suggest. Is not the common sense understanding of how the sentences came to be written quite simply this: the community (traditionally thought to be the Church in Rome) who first heard this Gospel read aloud contained two individuals called Alexander and Rufus. That these two actually existed. In, let us say, AD 70, an author is saying to his audience, 'You know those two forty- to fifty-year-olds who come to the Eucharist on Sunday – the pair of brothers – it was their father who helped to carry the Cross of Jesus.'

This makes us see that although the New Testament books are strange, and although they are not written as a modern writer would have composed them, they do contain evidence about the people who wrote them, and about the 'witnesses' who were still alive at the time of composition. Although, as we have perhaps said almost too often, they write about *Jesus* in a way which makes it all but impossible to 'deconstruct' the Scriptural tropes, the symbolic language, they do not write in this way about the *witnesses*. And the strangest thing is that even very late works, such as the Fourth Gospel, claim to have been written by witnesses.

After the last Resurrection appearance in that Gospel, in which, to parallel the three-fold denial, Jesus draws from Peter a three-fold assertion that he loves the Lord, there is a paragraph which has puzzled almost every reader. I do not propose a solution to any of the puzzles which it creates. I merely quote it as a reminder that, even in, let us say, AD 90 or 100, if you think this was when this Gospel was written down, the claim was being made that the testimony on which the Gospel was based relied on evidence of those who had actually known Jesus, and been present at the crucial moments.

> Peter turned and saw the disciple whom Jesus loved following them; he was the one who had reclined next to Jesus at the supper and had said, 'Lord, who is it that is going to betray you?' When Peter saw him, he said to Jesus, 'Lord what about him?' Jesus said to him, 'If it is my will that he remain until I come, what is that to you? Follow me!' So the rumour spread in the community that this disciple would not die. Yet Jesus did not say to him that he would not die, but, 'If it is my will that he remain until I come, what is that to you?' This is the disciple who is testifying to these things and has written them, and we know that his testimony is true. [John 21:20–24]

Long books have been written about the problems thrown up by these words, and this is not a long book. But we cannot escape the fact that even the Fourth Gospel, crafted and 'literary' and symbol-burdened as it is, claims to have been the work of one or more people ('we know that his testimony...') relying on the witness-account

of the man who had reclined next to Jesus at the Supper. Though
the material, the matter, of the Gospels, is historically intractable, it
would be difficult to get closer to an ancient witness than this. And
it is noticeable how frequently, and in how many books, this claim of
eye-witness testimony is made. The Fourth Gospel claims from the
beginning to be the work of one who witnessed the actual, earthly
Jesus: 'we have seen his glory' [John 1:14], at the beginning, going
right through to the end – 'This is the disciple who is testifying
to these things and who has written them, and we know that his
testimony is true' [John 21:24].

While I was writing the last two or three pages, I opened my Bible
at Revelation, and an old letter from L. dropped out of it: she must
have written it to me over twenty years ago – from Ghent, where she
had gone to see the Altarpiece.

> There is such calm. Van Eyck has chosen to depict the Lamb
> upon the Throne on a summer day in Flanders, one of those
> still days when you can hear bees buzzing from afar. Very
> different from the rather raucous rendering of the medieval
> hymn 'Jerusalem the Golden', which has 'the song of them
> that triumph, the shout of them that feast'!
>
> If only I could get on with the Bible book! I stood in
> front of Van Eyck for about an hour this morning and will
> go back this afternoon. But two things remain with me from
> my first viewing: the first, as I have said, is the stillness. He
> has managed, in paint, to convey that wonderful line 'there

was silence in heaven for about half an hour' [Revelation 8:1].

The other thing is – the people! Who said the Western Front was intolerable because 'my dear, the noise! And the people!'? Van Eyck's heaven is beautiful not because of the lack of noise, but because of the presence of people. Do you remember Merton's 'Fourth and Walnut Revelation', when he had been living for a long time as a solitary, but in 1958 he had to go into Louisville, Kentucky, for a doctor's appointment? And on the corner of Fourth and Walnut, he had this 'revelation', a sense of oneness and love with all the people around him?

You know The Book – I mean, My Book – the book I haven't written. (If I gave you my notes, maybe you could see a way of making it into a book?) Well, in that Book which never seems to get written... I have this idea of the Bible not being a dead text which is incomprehensible to us because it was written so long ago; and not a weapon to use against people we disapprove of... but this richly cherished source of inspiration to so many people! And it is partly the gift of God to his people, but also the gift of the people to God. They have fashioned it. They have read it. Wallace Stevens discarding the false images and reworking language itself is there in the crowd of witnesses, with Martin Luther King, and Gandhi, who remade and rediscovered the Bible's spirit of prophecy, and the Emperor Justinian rebuilding Holy Wisdom as the greatest setting for liturgy the world had ever seen! And Thomas Merton is there, with his highly charged sense of the Holy Spirit... and the people of South Africa are there, who chose to be reconciled to their persecutors rather than massacring them; and Solzhenitsyn is there, with all the twenty million who suffered with him in the Gulag – and Akhmatova is there with her hymn of Requiem for the uncounted millions who died in the camps... Each of them, like Alyosha the Baptist in *Ivan Denisovich*, making the Bible anew for themselves, reciting it, living it, letting it change their lives, and in their turn *changing it*. Probably very sentimental, and you'd do it differently – and maybe a drier, more academic approach would be better? Perhaps something on Farrer/Ramsey and their readings of the Apocalypse?

In AD 70, the Roman armies occupied Jerusalem and destroyed it. Those who believed themselves to be living in the 'last days' must have felt vindicated. And those Jews who had engaged with the very earliest Christians, Jews and Gentiles, must have been given pause. For the destructive Roman soldiery had enacted what Paul and the Letter to the Hebrews had been saying a whole decade earlier: the old ceremonies, the old animal sacrifices, the cherished liturgy of the Temple could no longer be celebrated. History had supplanted them.

In the decades after the cataclysmic events of AD 70, the Jews scattered to join the Diaspora in North Africa, in Asia Minor and in Rome. In Asia Minor, one of their leaders was called John. He was a Jew who was steeped in the old calendar of Feasts – Tabernacles, Lights and Passover.

Who was he? We do not know. But there are clues. In about 190, there was a man called Polycrates of Ephesus who wrote a letter about a long-standing quarrel between the Church of Rome and the Churches of Asia about the date of Easter. The Eastern Christians celebrated Easter on the fourteenth day of the Jewish month Nisan, whatever day of the week that was – because it was the Passover. The Roman Christians had begun to celebrate Easter on the first Sunday after 14th Nisan.

Polycrates belonged to a Christian family with memories of the very earliest Christians. He wished to make it clear to the Romans that his conservatism about the date of Easter was based on near-personal knowledge with the apostles themselves. Philip, who was one of the Twelve, had settled in Hierapolis with two of his daughters, and Polycrates gives more than a hint that he is descended from a third daughter. (There were four girls, according to Acts 21:9 – they 'prophesied'.) He also spoke of 'John, he who leaned back on the Lord's breast, who was a priest wearing the high priestly frontlet (*to petalon*), both witness (*martus*) and teacher. He has fallen asleep at Ephesus.'

Polycrates named seven great Christian luminaries, all of whom kept Easter on Nisan 14th and with all of whom he claimed to be personally connected. John is the one who interests us here.

Describing John as the one who had 'leaned on the Lord's breast' is a clear reference to the tradition that on the night before Jesus's death, the disciple 'whom he loved' leaned on his breast [John 13:23; 21:20]. He is claiming that this Beloved Disciple observed Easter on 14th Nisan.

In Acts 4, we read of disputes between the Temple hierarchy and the followers of Jesus who proclaimed that he had risen from the dead. 'The next day their rulers, elders and scribes assembled in Jerusalem, with Annas the high priest and Caiaphas, John and Alexander, and all who were of the high-priestly family.' [Acts 4:5–6] It is only speculation, but I find extremely convincing the suggestion made by Richard Bauckham that this John, of high-priestly family, is our man. It is clear that Polycrates did not believe that the author of the Fourth Gospel was John the Son of Zebedee, that is, one of the Twelve. The Beloved Disciple was none other than a son of the High Priest, one who was himself destined one day to wear the *petalon*, the high-priestly frontlet.

If this is true, of course, it suggests that the high priestly family themselves were eventually convinced of the truth of the apostolic teaching, and came to believe in the Resurrection. Either way, we have Polycrates's authority for believing that the daughters of Philip, with their gift of prophecy, were originally members of the Jerusalem Church and moved to Asia where 'they may well have brought Jewish and Jewish Christian apocalyptic traditions from Palestine into the circle of Christian prophets in Asia'.

The point is, not that one has to accept Polycrates/Bauckham's theory of the identity of John, but that these books did not come from nowhere. The Book of Revelation is a testimony, a witness, made in the closing years of the first century by one who, even if he did not himself belong to the first generation of Christian believers, was closely in touch with those who did: and whose testimony is not that of the Victorian 'Historical Jesus' or 'Jesus of History'. Not at all.

⁓

'SEE, THE HOME OF GOD IS AMONG MORTALS.'
[Revelation 21:3]

⁓

Opening a book can sometimes be a life-changing experience. In Jeanette Winterson's wonderful autobiography, she recorded, 'I asked my mother why we couldn't have books and she said, "The trouble with a book is that you never know what's in it until it's too late."'

No depiction of a reading experience is more dramatic, more terrible, more explosive, than the opening of the scroll in Revelation.

In the Authorized Version, the passage reads:

> And I saw in the right hand of him that sat on the throne a book written within and on the backside, sealed with seven seals. And I saw a strong angel proclaiming with a loud voice, Who is worthy to open the book, and to loose the seals thereof? And no one in heaven, nor in earth, neither under the earth, was able to open the book, neither to look thereon. And I wept much, because no one was found worthy to open and read the book, neither to look thereon. And one of the elders saith unto me, Weep not: behold, the Lion of the tribe of Juda, the root of David, hath prevailed to open the book, and to loose the seven seals thereof. [Revelation 5:1–5]

The word used in Greek is *biblion*. The Book in the vision is a scroll-book, such as would have been seen in the cupboards of synagogues throughout this period, and not a codex, such as you are holding in your hand – either made of paper and card, or a simulated codex in electronic form.

The Book in this vision contains visions of What is To Come. It is a secret book, sealed with seven seals, and its interpretation is impossible for those who do not have eyes to see.

The only one worthy to open the seals is he who is seated upon the Throne. We have now become accustomed to Bible reading, so that we know how Scriptural writers, including the writers of New Testament Letters and Gospels, build up their narratives and effects by constant allusion to earlier Scriptures. In this Revelation, this Book about Reading a Book, the Book which Cannot Be Opened, there is a thick density of allusion. It is a unique book, a book without parallel in the New Testament. But it is also a book which gathers up many other experiences of Jewish Apocalypse. In some of these texts, such as the Book of Jubilees, and 1 Enoch, the visionary consults 'heavenly tablets' which contain secrets of the future. In the opening of the Book of Ezekiel, [1:4–14] the seer confronted four living creatures with the faces of a lion, ox, eagle and man. Here they are again, in Revelation, though with crucial variations. In the Book of Daniel, the prophet is called upon to interpret divine secrets and oracles. In the last such scene, as Belshazzar, the King of Babylon, and his court are blasphemously quaffing from the sacred vessels stolen from the Temple at Jerusalem, mysterious writing appears on the wall. Only Daniel can interpret the strange words – MENE, MENE, TEKEL and PARSIN – which prophesy the doom of Babylon and the imminent Persian invasion. In Daniel 7, the prophet has a vision in which the Ancient of Days is seated upon his throne, and one like a son of man comes down from the clouds of heaven to be given glory and kingship. He needs the help of heavenly visitants to determine what the vision means.

Undoubtedly, the seer who wrote Revelation has such passages from the older Scriptures in mind.

Austin Farrer, in his commentary, wrote:

> What book is it? The setting is a heavenly synagogue, where Christ alone is able to open the Divine Law. But at the same time, the setting is that of Ezekiel's first vision; Christ's is that divine hand which spreads the book of prophecy before the eyes of his prophetic servant. Yet again, the setting is that of Daniel's seventh chapter. It is a heavenly court; the 'books are opened' that judgement may be pronounced in favour of the Saints of the Most High. What, then, does Christ open? Is it the Torah? Is it prophecy? Is it judgement? And how can one book be all three? It is more; it is THE BOOK, it is all that a heavenly book can be, all that there is for Christ to unseal. It is what is meant when the Fourth Evangelist writes: '*No man has seen God* at any time; the Only Begotten who is in the bosom of the Father, he has expounded.'

Austin Farrer was an academic priest who spent all his professional life in Oxford, first as Chaplain of Trinity College, and later as Warden of Keble College until his death in 1968. He was a great pioneer of the method of reading the Bible which has largely guided this book of mine – inspiring, among hundreds of other pupils, my wife R.'s aunt Aileen Guilding to write her book *The Fourth Gospel and Jewish*

Worship. For Farrer, described by Rowan Williams as 'possibly the greatest Anglican mind of the twentieth century', the Scriptures were both literary constructs and saving texts, aglow with living fire.

Academic theologians have seemed, roughly speaking, in my experience to fall into three categories. There were the ones who, having taken the Bible to pieces, found themselves without faith, and who continued to study it, aridly, as an academic discipline. If they had ever once heard the music of the spheres, they were now deaf to it. Often angered at their loss of faith, they were frequently hostile to the texts they studied, and determined to reduce or ridicule them.

Then there were those who kept their faith and their academic life in separate compartments. They continued to practise one or other version of Christianity on Sundays, and on Monday morning returned to accept the secularist agenda of the often heavyweight academics in my first category. These second-category divines were divided souls. A subsection of this category, perhaps the strangest of all, were those who practised all sorts of intellectual contortions to persuade themselves that certain undemonstrable propositions were true – for example, that the Last Supper was a Passover Meal, rather than merely accepting the Passover symbolism of the Eucharist and acknowledging that we do not know when the Last Supper was celebrated.

Then there was a (nowadays much smaller) category of theologian of whom Farrer, in modern Britain, was the Prince: those who recognized the Bible for what it was, who were entirely open and honest in their exegesis, but who never lost their awestruck consciousness of what they were studying. Farrer was in some ways a very rigorous, almost devastating analyst of Scriptural texts. He was also something of a mystic, a holy man, a man of God.

I packed his book on Revelation, *A Rebirth of Images*, to read on the train to Belgium and set off, on a very raw March day a couple of years ago. It was just impulse which took me. I thought that if I visited Ghent before Easter, I should be able to see the great altarpiece without having to battle my way through the crowds.

This, as it turned out, was a little optimistic. I arrived in the early afternoon. Flecks of sleet were falling from a lead-grey sky, and, having left my luggage at the modest hotel, I approached the cathedral, St Bavo, through a swarm of Japanese visitors. I had only a couple of days, and I intended to do nothing with my waking time other than look at this remarkable artwork, which I had been studying in books for a week.

On that first visit, about an hour before the cathedral closed for visitors, I was unable to get very near the masterpiece. Several guided tours were being told about it in different languages, including German, Japanese and American English – how it had been begun by Hubert van Eyck, who died in 1426, and completed by his brother Jan, how it had been commissioned for a rich Flemish merchant, and how, before the Reformation, the twelve separate panels were protected by panels which opened and shut by clockwork, and played music as they came open. The guides pointed out Adam and Eve in the top left and right panels, the angelic choirs in the next, and the great central panel at the top, flanked by one of the Virgin and one of St John, of the figure of God himself in a tiara, the three-tiered crown representing his triune nature.

It was easy to see, even during this first visit, how completely this painting embodied L.'s idea for her unwritten, and perhaps unwriteable, book. Reading is always a two-way process, even if you are reading a newspaper or a cheap crime story: there is the process of you absorbing the text, and of the text itself working some performative act, however briefly, upon the reader, amusing, boring, scaring the reader, and making her or him a different person. When the Reformation came to Europe, the Bible became a thing solely to be read, and printing created the illusion that it was a book like all other books, which could be placed on a library shelf. In the years before the Reformation, however, it was always clear that the Bible reads us as much as we read the Bible. It takes us into an imaginative world. It fills our minds with images of great potency which stay unexploded and unexplained in the mind for years before coming to life.

The Van Eycks' masterpiece belongs to this last phase of human imaginative history before the invention of printing and the fissiparation of Europe. Literacy, which is essential when reading most books, is not necessarily an advantage to us when reading the Bible. We need to recover the capacity to absorb images, and this is what the Ghent Altarpiece so strikingly does.

I went back the next morning, and was part of the first swarm of visitors allowed into the chapel. When looking at the reproductions of the altarpiece, I had never taken any notice of the font-like well in the foreground. Around the fountain are the words 'HIC EST FONS AQUAE VITAE PROCEDENS DE SEDE DEI ET AGNI' – 'This is the fountain of the water of life, proceeding out of the throne of God and of the Lamb'.

Farrer, whom I had been reading in my rather dingy hotel, had the idea that the Revelation/Apocalypse was the first book written by the Elder John. He was clearly a Jewish exile, presumably from Jerusalem – Bauckham speculates that he was actually a former priest of the Temple or even High Priest. He had jurisdiction, as a Christian archbishop, over seven churches of Asia and he had evidently been exiled – presumably during a Roman persecution following the destruction of Jerusalem – to the island of Patmos, where the vision occurred. Farrer then imagines that, after the fireworks of the Apocalypse, St John wrote the quieter version of the same story – his Gospel.

Many New Testament scholars have questioned whether the two books have the same authorship, but they do employ noticeably similar imagery – for example, the Lamb of God is a central image to both. Standing before the Ghent Altarpiece, I realized what the font-like structure was, from which flowed the waters of life.

'It is I, Jesus, who sent my angel to you with this testimony for the churches. I am the root and the descendant of David, the bright morning star.' The Spirit and the Bride say, 'Come.' And let everyone who hears say, 'Come.' And let everyone who is thirsty come. Let anyone who wishes take the water of life as a gift. [Revelation 22:16–17]

The woman said to him, 'Sir, you have no bucket and the well is deep. Where do you get that living water? Are you greater than our ancestor Jacob, who gave us the well, and with his sons and his flocks drank from it?' Jesus said to her, 'Everyone who drinks of this water will be thirsty again, but those who drink of the water that I will give will never be thirsty. The water I will give will become in them a spring of water gushing up to eternal life.' [John 4:11–14]

I had returned in my mind to Nablus, and in a sense my journey around the Bible was all but complete.

The Christian Bible has travelled a long way from the Garden of Eden, where two beings appeared, by virtue of the fact that Almighty God decided to make 'humankind in our image' [Genesis 1:26]. We have passed through the entire history of Judaism, from its origins at the time of the Babylonian exile, its mythologies of ancestral desert-wanderings, its building of temples and its setting up of ritual observances. Following the catastrophe of the destruction of Jerusalem in AD 70, religion itself, in its liturgical form, appeared to have been wiped off the board.

All those rules – about how, and when, and how many animals could be slaughtered; how this or that ritual impurity could be washed away; all the priestly and high-priestly rituals; all the sacred vessels, all the scrolls and books, and candlesticks, all the service books, all the musical instruments – are no more.

Perhaps the most imaginative feature of the Seer's vision in the Apocalypse is that in the New Jerusalem, the heavenly Jerusalem of his imagining, here too there is no religion. In the new dispensation, there is no more Shiite versus Sunni, no Buddhist versus Hindu, nor Catholic versus Protestant. 'I saw no temple in the city, for its temple is the Lord God Almighty and the Lamb. And the city has no need of sun or moon to shine on it, for the glory of God is its light, and its lamp is the Lamb. The nations will walk by its light, and the kings of the earth will bring their glory into it.' [Revelation 21:22–24]

In other words, the condition of humanity which was envisaged in the very first chapter of Genesis has been achieved. Men and women and children are made in God's image. The Law had been an attempt to cleanse humanity of its sins and flaws, but it could not do so.

> For you have no delight in sacrifice; if I were to give a burnt offering, you would not be pleased. The sacrifice acceptable to God is a broken spirit; a broken and contrite heart, O God, you will not despise. [Psalm 51:16–17]

> I will remove from your body the heart of stone and give you a heart of flesh. [Ezekiel 36:26]

> The days are surely coming, says the Lord, when I will make a new covenant with the house of Israel and the house of Judah ... I will put my law within them, and I will write it on their hearts [Jeremiah 31:31,33].

Christ did not come into the world to found a religion, but to make 'religions' superfluous.

On my last visit to the altarpiece, just after an unappetising brunch, the chapel had filled up, and was almost alarmingly full. I tried to concentrate on the sedate crowds of elders in Van Eyck's masterpiece, but there were too many people behind, and in front of me.

I thought, there are different ways of reading the Bible, and not all of them involve sitting down on your own and turning the pages of a book.

The Bible is the Book of the People, and we understand it by listening to what other people have made of it. Some of these people are so different from us that it is quite inconceivable that we shall ever think in exactly their way. This does not mean we have nothing to learn from them. You do not have to eat the food of a different ethnicity every day of your life, but life would be dull if you had never sampled how the Lebanese, or the Goans, or the Italians like to cook. Likewise, the neo-Platonic philosophers and theologians of the early Church, or the Scholastics of the high Middle Ages, or the neo-Hegelians of the nineteenth century had mindsets so different from ours that we should have to perform mental contortions if we shared all their ways of looking at the world. This does not mean we have nothing in common with them – they were human too, and some of their insights can help us.

Just as I turned to go – the corner of my eye glimpsed a familiar head over the shoulders and backpacks of my swarming tourist-companions. The tilt of the head, the brindled hair, the sheer height, the bottle-glass thick specs were unmistakable. So was the smile. Often L.'s smile was annoying – in life – but on this occasion, it seemed merely comforting. I blinked, I straightened up my gaze to see her properly. Strangely, it was no more, nor less, surprising to see her here, after death, than it was to meet her in the haphazard unplanned method of all our previous meetings. But as I looked for her in the crowd, she was gone, and I was unable to decide, through all the hotel afternoon, when I finished

Farrer and relapsed into a crossword puzzle, whether I had seen her, or only imagined her.

The next day was Palm Sunday and I returned to the cathedral to hear the whole of a Passion narrative (the chapters of one of the four Gospels describing the trial, torture and death of Jesus) sung by a group of different cantors. It is said that the chants used for this rendition derive from the music of the Temple in Jerusalem. Whether or not this is true, it is an extremely ancient chant, and the musical setting of the Gospel narrative, and the fact that we were listening to it collectively, rather than reading it on our own at home, made it much more vivid. I was not carried away by any mystic 'experience', but I was moved in my heart; for I realized with greater force than I had ever realized before that, merely because the text sung was a literary 'construct', this in no way diminished its authenticity. Dissect it for historical evidence, and it would simply remain a handful of dead shards on a laboratory bench. Sing it together among a crowd of the faithful, and there seems no good reason not to recognize it for what it is: the testimony of the whole Church, living and dead. 'They compelled a passer-by, who was coming in from the country, to carry his cross; it was Simon of Cyrene, the father of Alexander and Rufus. . .' [Mark 15:21]

My eyes wandered from face to face in the congregation. The line is unbroken throughout the generations. Every Sunday since Alexander and Rufus went to the Eucharist in Rome, some group of Christians had been meeting for the same rite, to share in the same Mystery. When the chanting of the Passion was over, I stayed to hear that Fifth

Gospel which I had heard when I visited the convent near Salisbury, with its great catalogue of witnesses. *John the Baptist, Stephen, Matthias, Barnabas, Ignatius, Alexander, Marcellinus, Peter, Felicity, Perpetua, Agatha, Lucy, Agnes, Cecilia, Anastasia and all your saints...*

This miscellaneous Belgian congregation contained many foreign tourists from, I should guess, four continents. The liturgy in which they took part proclaimed the presence of the Risen Jesus Christ in the broken bread and the shared cup. Their actions, words and beliefs were in essence the same as those practised by the congregation which had included Rufus and Alexander in Rome, within memory of the man who had helped to carry Christ's Cross. For hundreds of years before there was – as such – a book you could call the Bible, there were people passing on the tradition to the next generation. Alexander and Rufus. John who leaned on the bosom of the Lord at the Supper. As in any tradition conveyed by ritual and speech, there was a Chinese whispers effect; but the essence of it was very simple: the Crucified Lord rose. He returned to the Father in Glory. He left to his people his presence in the loaves. The loaves are his body. The people too are his body.

These people came before the Book. The Book is theirs. The Church came first – the gathering for the liturgy. Decades before there were written Gospels, Christians met together, sharing their faith in the Resurrection of Jesus Christ in the Breaking of Bread – the Eucharist, the Holy Communion, the Liturgy, the Mass. They had a church order – elders or bishops and deacons – which they believed descended directly from the Twelve, chosen by Jesus himself. When it came to be written, after the Fall of Jerusalem, the Gospel tradition was spare. The writers did not write as modern biographers would have written. They told us almost nothing of a 'biographical' character about Jesus or about his mother Mary. A few stories about the infancy (the more fantastical Gospels, describing a wonder-working child, were rejected from the Canon); a selection of stories about his healing powers; a selection of his stories and the core of his teaching – to die to self, to distrust riches and hierarchy, to love one another. This meagre tradition was deemed by the early Church to be enough, and it was as if they did not want more than enough. The Johannine tradition – that it was more blessed not to have seen, and to have believed – is found in the other traditions too. This alone must surely give a sceptic pause. You would expect the tradition, if it were all fabrication, to make tall stories taller, and to have repeated wonders and miracles, rather than the tradition of Jesus, when alive, urging his disciples to keep his identity as the Messiah a secret, and when dead and risen, appearing in the most ambiguous ways – in at least three of the stories not even being recognized by those who had known him best. In the earliest of all the accounts, of the discovery of the empty tomb, that of Mark, the friends of Jesus flee from the empty tomb because they were afraid [Mark 16:8] and that is the end of the story. Artful indeed if it was all invention; understandable, if the sense of the risen Christ in the early Church was so palpable, in the gathering of the faithful, and in the Breaking of Bread, that they did not even need the reassurance of Resurrection stories.

The Books which the elders and scholars chose to put into our Bible, and those they chose to reject, when it was being compiled during the fourth to fifth century, were a human choice, though the collection has a mysterious wholeness and meaning. Frequent and deep reading of the Bible will not convince any reader that all of it is true, in the sense that literalists would use the term, but they will convince any imaginative reader to understand life and language anew through its pages. The Bible reminds us that all human language is metaphor, all expressions of metaphysical truth, or scientific truth, are in one sense mythological. The Bible does not compete with the metaphors of Science or Literature or Philosophy, but its own metaphors can inform life. The People who produced the Book had their own philosophies, their own understandings of science, which are not ours. The Book mysteriously remains, and whether we hear it used in liturgy or read it in private, it retains its undying luminosity.

Through all those two thousand years or so of experience, the understanding of the world, of time, of history and science, has varied enormously from culture to culture, and from age to age. The Bible, which became part of that culture after it had been formed into a single book, has also been understood and interpreted, from age to age, in quite different ways. Fundamentalist attacks upon it, and fundamentalist defences of it, have both, in their eerily similar ways, tried to make it into an ersatz Bible, an unchanging thing, graven in stone, stern and brainless, a lumpen edifice with THOU SHALT NOT carved over the door. It never was, and never has been, such a book. It contains much that is puzzling, much that is repellent, much that is alarming, as does the human soul. It is also an incomparably rich collection of writings, brought together by Providence to form a single whole, which both reflects and enlightens each life that reads in it deeply. It is the text of all texts, the book which underlies almost all the great works of Western literature from the time of its compilation, until the Enlightenment and beyond. Without a knowledge of it, the great portion of Western architecture is incomprehensible. It is the key which unlocks the work of nearly all the painters, from Giotto to Blake. It is the libretto of Bach and Haydn and Beethoven. On battlefields, on deathbeds, in hospital wards and private households rich and poor, its leaves have been turned, its pages opened, its well-known words have nourished and sustained countless human lives. In its poetry, men and women have found echoes of their own heartbreak, their own doubt, their own dejection, their own sins, as well as a staff to comfort and a light to guide. When Sir Walter Scott was dying, he asked his son-in-law to read to him. The son-in-law, Lockhart, who knew that Sir Walter had written so many books, and acquired so many more for his magnificent library, asked him – from which book? He said, 'Need you ask – there is but one.'

EPILOGUE

Q UEEN VICTORIA DISLIKED being addressed as if she were a public meeting. I hope, if you have read to the end of this book, that you feel that you have been having a gentle conversation, and not that you have been harangued.

It would not be quite honest, however, if I pretended that the book had no agenda. I hope that at least one fundamentalist – either a Christian or an atheist one – will have paused and wondered whether they have been reading the Bible in the wrong way. I have hinted many times in this book that much which is most rich in the Western cultural inheritance was inspired by the Bible – campaigns of political freedom, poetry old and new, painting, music. It is an obvious point in a way, but is the reason for it obvious?

Biblical fundamentalism, espoused so clumsily by believers and unbelievers, sees 'the Bible' as a shopping list of bossy assertions: take your choice, we all know what this way of reading Scripture enjoins. The anti-Godders read the Bible and see only poison, because they obediently read it in the way that the religious fundamentalists tell them it is to be read. Here is a book, both sides of this ludicrous argument believe, which asserts as a scientific fact that the world came into being in the space of six days. Or here is a book which condemns homosexuality (and most other forms of sexual activity). While I was preparing this book for press, I heard on the news that an Islamic court in Iran had condemned someone for not believing that Daniel was an historical figure who really spent a night in an actual lion's den.

It is easy to feel superior to the bigots in the Middle East who insist upon Biblical fundamentalism. But many of the secularists who reject our religious heritage make the same crass mental errors.

There was a reason, once the Christian Bible had been printed and become a book in Europe in the sixteenth century, why it inspired even more works of art than it had done in its previous fifteen hundred years of history. There is a reason why the Reformation morphed into the Romantic Movement, and why figures such as William Blake and William Wordsworth derived so much of their inspiration from the Bible.

And that is a very simple reason. The Bible – multifarious in its authors and origins – is itself a work of the imagination. It is not all written in poetry, but it is much more like poetry than it is like any other form of literature. The act of creation was not finished when the first scribe wrote the words of Scripture on a piece of papyrus. Biblical creativity only began with this process, and unfolded with each reading, each repetition, each understanding by a human being, many of them hearing the words in translation from the original Hebrew or Latin or Greek; some of them hearing because they could not read, but still absorbing into their imaginative life the living Word which the Bible was and is.

Stand outside a great church – for example, Bath Abbey, where you can see, carved in stone, a medieval depiction of the angels of God ascending and descending to earth by ladders. In the reign of Henry VII, in 1499, Bishop King had a dream in which he saw angels ascending and descending; and he heard a voice saying, 'Let a King restore the church' – which he did. King's dream was itself a reference to the dream which Israel/Jacob had in the Book of Genesis. It is one of the most sublime images ever conceived by the human imagination of the possibility either (as in this story) through dreams and the subconscious, or through other channels – love, music, silence, walking, nature, or in the case of a bishop in 1499, sleeping and thinking of architecture – of mortal men and women feeling themselves in touch with something beyond material experience.

The secular fundamentalist might feel that the angels on the west front of Bath Abbey should by rights be chipped off, or covered with a layer of concrete, lest they confuse the unwary into supposing that an early Tudor bishop had actually seen visitors from outer space, or that the ancestor of the Jews in the mists of time had seen spacemen coming out of the sky on extra-terrestrial ladders. (This is, as a matter of fact, what some modern proponents of Scientology do believe!)

This fundamentalist way of reading the west front of Bath Abbey is, surely, however, not merely stupid, but perverse. Most normal surveyors of those medieval stone angels would see them as potent symbols, and would recall the passage of Genesis to which they refer. Like so much in what is perhaps the richest of all Biblical texts, it seeks not to assert, but to question, to nudge the imagination in the direction of uncertainty, to recognize that life cannot always be judged by appearances. 'Then Jacob woke from his sleep and said, "Surely the Lord is in this place – and I did not know it!"' [Genesis 28:16]

NOTES

Except where otherwise stated, the Biblical quotations are taken from *The New Oxford Annotated Bible*, edited by Bruce M. Metzger and Roland E. Murphy, New York, Oxford University Press, 1991. In Chapter Five, on Job, most of the Biblical quotations are taken from the Authorized Version (1611).

Factual references are all drawn, unless otherwise stated, from *The Oxford Companion to the Bible*, edited by Bruce M. Metzger and Michael D. Coogan, New York/Oxford, Oxford University Press, 1993.

2 THE VULGATE OF EXPERIENCE

'Huitzilopochtli is as magnificently forgotten...' H. L. Mencken, 'Memorial Service', in *H. L. Mencken on Religion*, edited by S. T. Joshi, Amherst, NY, Prometheus Books, 2002, p. 293.

'The death of one god...' Wallace Stevens, 'Notes Toward a Supreme Fiction', *Collected Poetry and Prose*, New York, The Library of America (Alfred A. Knopf Inc.), 1997, p. 329.

'The Bible is held together...' Northrop Frye, *Words with Power*, San Diego/New York/London, Harcourt Brace Jovanovich, 1990, p. 102.

'*Das Werdende, das ewig wirkt und lebt...*' Goethe, *Faust: Part One*, Prologue in Heaven (author's translation).

Here, in this story of Jacob's Dream... John Skinner DD, *A Critical and Exegetical Commentary on Genesis*, Edinburgh, T. & T. Clark, 1980 (first published 1910), p. 376.

'You know, next year in Jerusalem...' This dates the conversation to 1995.

'Transparent man...' Stevens, 'On the Way to the Bus', *Collected Poetry and Prose*, p. 472.

'The milkman came...' Stevens, 'Les Plus Belles Pages', *Collected Poetry and Prose*, p. 222.

'God does not exist, he is eternal...' Kierkegaard, *The Last Years: Journals 1853–55*, edited and translated by Ronald Gregor Smith, Collins, 1965, p. 155.

'The eye's plain version...' Stevens, 'An Ordinary Evening in New Haven', *Collected Poetry and Prose*, p. 397.

'The poem is the cry...' Ibid.

'The summer night...' Stevens, 'The House Was Quiet and the World Was Calm', *Collected Poetry and Prose*, p. 331.

'Clear your mind of cant...' James Boswell, *The Life of Samuel Johnson*, Oxford, Oxford University Press, 1946, II, p. 496.

3 PROPHETS

'If my mental processes...' J. B. S. Haldane, *Possible Worlds*, quoted in C. S. Lewis, *Miracles*, London, Geoffrey Bles, 1947, p. 28.

'By trusting to argument...' Lewis, *Miracles*, p. 28.

King saw political and social events. . . Richard Lischer, *The Preacher King: Martin Luther King, Jr. and the Word that Moved America*, New York/Oxford, Oxford University Press, 1995, p. 4.

'If we are wrong. . .' Martin Luther King Jr, Address to the first Montgomery Improvement Association Mass Meeting, 5 December 1955, http://mlk-kppo1.stanford.edu/index.php/encyclopedia/ documentsentry/the_addres_to_the_first_montgomery_improvement_ association_mia_mass_meeting/ (retrieved 11 November 2014).

'You *can't* hem him. . .' Lischer, *The Preacher King*, p. 161.

'We will march around. . .' Lischer, Ibid., p. 248.

'Hebrew scholars contend. . .' Lischer, Ibid., p. 177.

'After the first temple. . .' William M. Schniedewind, *The Word of God in Transition: From Prophet to Exegete in the Second Temple Period*, Sheffield, Sheffield Academic Press, 1995, p. 15.

Whether you take the view. . . Schniedewind defends the earlier dating. Thomas L. Thompson, *The Bible in History* (London, Jonathan Cape, 1999), and Philip R. Davies, *In Search of 'Ancient Israel'* (Sheffield, Sheffield Academic Press, 1995), are representatives of the late dating theory.

'orality was. . .' Schniedewind, *The Word of God in Transition*, p. 119.

The Rabbis believed. . . William M. Schniedewind, *How the Bible Became a Book: The Textualization of Ancient Israel*, Cambridge, Cambridge University Press, 2004, p. 15, *passim*.

'The Christian. . .' Piers McGrandle, *Trevor Huddleston: Turbulent Priest*, London, Continuum, 2004, p. 123.

'It is this mystery. . .' *Ibid.*, p. 125.

'The Baptist was reading. . .' Alexander Solzhenitsyn, *One Day in the Life of Ivan Denisovich*, London, Everyman, 1995, p. 23.

4 HOLY WISDOM

'**whenever one enters...**' *Procopius on Buildings*, edited and translated by H. B. Dewing, Loeb Classical Library, London, William Heinemann, and New York, G. P. Putnam's Sons, 1914-54, III, p. 389.

'**we knew not whether...**' *The Russian Primary Chronicle: Laurentian Text*, translated and edited by Samuel Hazzard Cross and Olgerd P. Shobowitz-Wetzor, Cambridge, MA: Mediaeval Academy of America, 1953, p. 111.

'**At your mystical supper...**' Quoted in Derek Krueger, 'Christian Piety and Practice in the Sixth Century', in *The Cambridge Companion to the Age of Justinian*, edited by Michael Maas, Cambridge, Cambridge University Press, 2005, p. 292.

'**The *Logos* is no longer...**' Edward Gibbon, *The History of the Decline and Fall of the Roman Empire*, edited by David Womersley, London, Allen Lane, 1994, I.xxi, p. 782.

'***Cesare fui e son Iustiniano...***' Dante, *The Divine Comedy*, translated by Robin Kirkpatrick, London, Penguin Books, 2007, *Paradiso* VI.10–12, p. 50.

'**The vain titles...**' Gibbon, II.xliv, *History of the Decline and Fall of the Roman Empire*, II.xliv, p. 778.

'**The satirical historian...**' Ibid., II.xl, p. 565.

'**From his elevation...**' Ibid., II.xl, p. 561.

'**Two things fill the mind...**' Immanuel Kant, *Kritik der praktischen Vernunft* (*Critique of Practical Reason*), Werke in Sechs Bänden, im Insel Verlag, 1956 Band IV, 300.

'**The Greek word...**' Gibbon, *History of the Decline and Fall of the Roman Empire*, I.xxi, p. 782.

'**And this failure...**' Rose Macaulay, *The Towers of Trebizond*, London, Collins, 1956, p. 159.

5 JOB

'Lloyd-Jones reminds us. . .' Sophocles, *Tragedies (In Two Volumes)*, translated by Hugh Lloyd-Jones, Cambridge, MA, Harvard University Press, 1994, I, p. 1.

'I know of no other Christianity. . .' Quoted in Andrew Wright, *Blake's Job: A Commentary*, Oxford, The Clarendon Press, 1972, p. 51.

'May God us keep. . .' William Blake, *The Poetry and Prose of William Blake*, edited by Geoffrey Keynes, London, The Nonesuch Press, 1939, p. 862.

'In the last plate. . .' Northrop Frye, 'The Keys to the Gates', in James V. Logan et al. (eds), *Some British Romantics: A collection of essays*, Columbus, OH, Ohio State University Press, 1966, p. 40.

Which academic examiner. . . http://en.wikipedia.org/wiki/Christ_myth_ theory#Thomas_L._Thompson (retrieved 18 November 2014).

6 LIVING IN A METAPHOR: PSALMS

'*Entre deux hommes. . .*' Simone Weil, *Cahiers*, Paris, Gallimard, 2006, VI, p. 302.

'Here we are astonished. . .' Simone Pétrement, *Simone Weil: A Life*, translated by Raymond Rosenthal, London/Oxford, Mowbray, 1977, p. 330.

'Love bade me welcome. . .' George Herbert, 'Love', *Complete Poems*, edited by John Tobin, Harmondsworth, Penguin, 1991, p. 178.

'*Iobs* number. . .' John Donne, in Izaak Walton, *The Lives of John Donne, Sir Henry Wotton, Richard Hooker, George Herbert and Robert Sanderson*, Oxford, Oxford World's Classics, 1927, p. 64.

'Joy, I did lock thee up. . .' Herbert, 'The Bunch of Grapes', *Complete Poems*, p. 119.

'The poet invents. . .' R. S. Thomas, *A Choice of George Herbert's Verse*, Faber & Faber, 1967, p. 15.

'Test me...' Mitchell Dahood SJ (editor and translator), *Psalms III*, New Haven, CT, Yale University Press, 2007, III.

The classic mythological expression... Plato, *The Republic*, from *The Dialogues of Plato*, translated by Benjamin Jowett, London, Sphere Books, 1970, IV.

'If I take wing...' Robert Alter, *The Book of Psalms. A Translation with Commentary*, New York, W. W. Norton, 2007, p. 203.

'Of whom can it more truly...' Thomas Merton, *Bread in the Wilderness*, London, Burns & Oates, 1976, p. 64.

'If you don't do so already...' J. R. R. Tolkien, *Letters of J. R. R. Tolkien*, edited by Humphrey Carpenter, London, George Allen & Unwin, 1981, p. 66.

'Man lives...' Northrop Frye, *The Great Code: The Bible and Literature*, London, Routledge & Kegan Paul, 1982, p. xviii.

The conundrum... For an excellent summary of the difficulties of investigating the origin of the Eucharist, see Robert J. Daly SJ, 'Eucharistic Origins: from the New Testament to the Liturgies of the Golden Age', in *Theological Studies* 66, 2005, p. 3 ff.

'the effect of...' Colin J. Humphreys, *The Mystery of the Last Supper: Reconstructing the Final Days of Jesus*, Cambridge, Cambridge University Press, 2011, p. 55.

'The only difference...' Richard Dawkins, quoted in Humphreys, *Mystery of the Last Supper*, p. 1.

'Insofar as the figure...' Thomas L. Brodie, *Beyond the Quest for the Historical Jesus: Memoir of a Discovery*, Sheffield, Sheffield Phoenix Press, 2012, p. 213.

'The tragedy with the quest...' Brodie, Ibid., p. 61.

'*Plagas, sicut Thomas*...' Thomas Aquinas, in *The Penguin Book of Latin Verse*, edited by Frederick Brittain, Harmondsworth, Penguin Books, 1962, p. 258.

'in testing the Gospels. . .' Brodie, *Beyond the Quest for the Historical Jesus*, p. 35.

Did not Paul. . . Many Christian scholars who do believe Paul existed question his authorship of Colossians.

'To say Jesus. . .' Brodie, *Beyond the Quest for the Historical Jesus*, p. xiv.

'Did it really happen?. . .' Brodie, Ibid., p. 106.

7 THE REBIRTH OF IMAGES

'A scene like. . .' Erich Auerbach, *Mimesis: The Representation of Reality in Western Literature*, translated by Willard R. Trask, Princeton, Princeton University Press, 1953, p. 45.

'John, he who leaned back. . .' Translation of Eusebius of Caesarea, quoted in Richard Bauckham, *Jesus and the Eyewitnesses: The Gospels as Eyewitness Testimony*, Grand Rapids, MI/Cambridge, William B. Eerdmans Publishing Company, 2006, p. 439.

'they may well. . .' Richard Bauckham, *The Climax of Prophecy: Studies on the Book of Revelation*, Edinburgh, T. & T. Clark, 1993, p. 87.

'I asked my mother. . .' Jeanette Winterson, *Why Be Happy When You Could Be Normal?*, London, Jonathan Cape, 2011, p. 33.

'What book is it?. . .' Austin Farrer, *A Rebirth of Images: The Making of St John's Apocalypse*, London, Dacre Press, 1949, p. 43.

SELECTED
READING LIST

Karen Armstrong, *The Great Transformation: The World in the Time of Buddha, Socrates, Confucius and Jeremiah*, London, Atlantic Books, 2006

Erich Auerbach, *Mimesis: The Representation of Reality in Western Literature*, translated by Willard R. Trask, Princeton, Princeton University Press, 1953

Timothy Barnes, *Constantine: Dynasty, Religion and Power in the Later Roman Empire*, Malden, MA/Oxford, Wiley-Blackwell, 2011

Richard Bauckham, *The Climax of Prophecy: Studies on the Book of Revelation*, Edinburgh, T. & T. Clark, 1993

Richard Bauckham, *Jesus and the Eyewitnesses: The Gospels as Eyewitness Testimony*, Grand Rapids, MI/Cambridge, William B. Eerdmans Publishing Company, 2006

William Blake, *The Poetry and Prose of William Blake*, edited by Geoffrey Keynes, London, The Nonesuch Press, 1939

Thomas L. Brodie, *Beyond the Quest for the Historical Jesus: Memoir of a Discovery*, Sheffield, Sheffield Phoenix Press, 2012

Dante, *The Divine Comedy – Inferno, Purgatorio and Paradiso* (3 volumes), translated by Robin Kirkpatrick, London, Penguin Books, 2007

Elisabeth Dhanens, *Van Eyck: The Ghent Altarpiece*, London, Allen Lane, 1973

Gregory Dix, *The Shape of the Liturgy*, London, Dacre Press, 1946

Austin Farrer, *A Rebirth of Images: The Making of St John's Apocalypse*, London, Dacre Press, 1949

Northrop Frye, *Fearful Symmetry: A Study of William Blake*, Princeton, Princeton University Press, 1947

Northrop Frye, *The Great Code: The Bible and Literature*, London, Routledge & Kegan Paul, 1982

Northrop Frye, *Words with Power: Being a Second Study of the Bible and Literature*, San Diego/New York/London, Harcourt Brace Jovanovich, 1990

Edward Gibbon, *The History of the Decline and Fall of the Roman Empire* (3 volumes), edited by David Womersley, London, Allen Lane, 1994

Aileen Guilding, *The Fourth Gospel and Jewish Worship*, Oxford, The Clarendon Press, 1960

George Herbert, *Complete Poems*, edited by John Tobin, Harmondsworth, Penguin, 1991

Colin J. Humphreys, *The Mystery of the Last Supper: Reconstructing the Final Days of Jesus*, Cambridge, Cambridge University Press, 2011

C. S. Lewis, *Miracles: A Preliminary Study*, London, Geoffrey Bles, 1942

Richard Lischer, *The Preacher King: Martin Luther King, Jr. and the Word that Moved America*, New York/Oxford, Oxford University Press, 1995

Alfred Loisy, *L'Evangile et l'Eglise*, Paris, Picard et fils, 1902

Michael Maas (editor), *The Cambridge Companion to the Age of Justinian*, Cambridge, Cambridge University Press, 2005

Rose Macaulay, *The Towers of Trebizond*, London, Collins, 1956

Piers McGrandle, *Trevor Huddleston: Turbulent Priest*, London, Continuum, 2004

Rowland Mainstone, *Hagia Sophia: Architecture, Structure and Liturgy of Justinian's Great Church*, London, Thames and Hudson, 1988

Thomas Merton, *Bread in the Wilderness*, London, Burns & Oates, 1976

Bruce Metzger and Michael D. Coogan (editors), *The Oxford Companion to the Bible*, New York/Oxford, Oxford University Press, 1993

Jürgen Moltmann, *The Crucified God: The Cross of Christ as the Foundation and Criticism of Christian Theology*, translated by R. A. Wilson and John Bowden, London, SCM Press, 2001

John Henry Newman, *An Essay on the Development of Christian Doctrine*, London, Longman, Green & Co., 1901 (first published 1845)

Dennis Nineham, *The Use and Abuse of the Bible: A Study of the Bible in an Age of Rapid Cultural Change*, London, Macmillan, 1976

The Psalms, A New Translation, London, Collins, 1983

William M. Schniedewind, *The Word of God in Transition: From Prophet to Exegete in the Second Temple Period*, Sheffield, Sheffield Academic Press, 1995

William M. Schniedewind, *How the Bible Became a Book: The Textualization of Ancient Israel*, Cambridge, Cambridge University Press, 2004

John Skinner DD, *A Critical and Exegetical Commentary on Genesis*, Edinburgh, T. & T. Clark, 1980 (first published 1910)

Sophocles, *Tragedies (In Two Volumes)*, translated by Hugh Lloyd-Jones, Cambridge, MA, Harvard University Press, 1994

Wallace Stevens, *Collected Poetry and Prose*, New York, The Library of America (Alfred A. Knopf Inc.), 1997

Thomas L. Thompson, *The Bible in History: How Writers Create a Past*, London, Jonathan Cape, 1999

J. R. R. Tolkien, *Letters of J. R. R. Tolkien*, edited by Humphrey Carpenter, London, George Allen & Unwin, 1981

PERMISSIONS